RANDOM HOUSE
**LARGE
PRINT**

ALSO BY TOM BROKAW
AVAILABLE FROM
RANDOM HOUSE LARGE PRINT

The Greatest Generation

NEVER GIVE UP

NEVER GIVE UP

A Prairie Family's Story

TOM BROKAW

RANDOM HOUSE
LARGE PRINT

To
Red and Jean Brokaw
and
Meredith, always

CONTENTS

Red and Jean on their wedding day

PREFACE

From the beginning, America has occupied a unique place in the long history of political and cultural challenges to survival.

From the Revolutionary War of 1776, through the Civil War; World War I; World War II, the greatest conflict in human history; and devastating economic and viral assaults, including the flu epidemic of 1918, the life span of this unique nation has depended on more than just armies and navies. It has depended on shared values prevailing against assaults on common destinies.

Now, in the twenty-first century, the unexpected and devastating presence of a sinister biological agent that has killed people, roiled the economy, and deeply divided common cause has done unprecedented damage to this precious nation. Simultaneously and unexpectedly, a new conflict broke out with an old adversary. Russia and its tyrannical leader attacked one of Europe's new democracies.

In these chaotic times, what can we learn from history?

As a citizen, husband, father, and grandfather, I have drawn on the lessons I absorbed of the struggles of the Great Depression, a great war, and the emergence of financial security from my working-class family. My parents' generation was grateful for new opportunities, but they never took the better times for granted. In their roles as parents and citizens, the later experiences of Vietnam and social and racial upheaval also imprinted in them fiscal and personal caution.

I never heard them complain about what fate had delivered to them as they made their way through hard times and the limited social programs available until the Great Society took hold.

The most enduring lesson I learned from them?

Never give up.

PART I

CHAPTER 1

Bristol,
South Dakota

IN THE LATE NINETEENTH CENTURY, in the Great
Plains of Middle America, the American savanna,
the land rush was on.

It was a vast swath of real estate that was low on
water and rich in challenges—from brutal winter
seasons to scorching summers. Until recently it had
been the home of enormous herds of antelope and
American bison, the magnificent beast prized for its
rich pelts and thick cuts of red meat.

After the Civil War and during the great migra-
tion of immigrants from northern Europe and
Scandinavia to America, that part of the United
States was also prized for two irresistible qualities:
Land was dirt cheap (or free), and there was lots of
it. America's flourishing railroad industry saw fresh
opportunity for new business, so it pushed into that
harsh but promising prairie.

My great-grandfather, R. P. Brokaw, left his Upstate

New York home after the Civil War and headed west seeking security as a farmer or innkeeper.

The Brokaws were Huguenots, enterprising Protestants who had fled France and taken up residence in Holland before coming to America, where many flourished in New York and New Jersey real estate, the arts, and civic affairs. But R. P. Brokaw took another route, not nearly as rewarding. R.P. went north, into the New York wilderness, where he opened a small market in the Finger Lakes region.

He was a quartermaster and clerk for the North in the Civil War, emerging with a modest pension to finance his trip to the new territories in the American West.

He rode the rails and farmed along the way until he reached what was to become the state of South Dakota. Founders of the Milwaukee Road railroad saw opportunity in the eagerness of the new immigrants to take advantage of land bargains. R.P. stopped in a new village of wooden shanties and primitive homes because it had a promising feature: a rail line north and south and one east and west.

A Milwaukee Road railroad developer had given these new villages British city names and this one was called Bristol. R.P. decided it needed overnight accommodations. He started with a tented commissary and then began constructing the first substantial building in town and called it The Brokaw House. R.P., his son William, and his daughter-in-law, Elizabeth, ran

The Brokaw House as a hotel, boardinghouse, and center of civic activity.

By 1889, South Dakota, with statehood, began to attract more settlers, but it remained a frontier.

William would meet incoming Milwaukee Road trains as they arrived on that stretch of the prairie. He would greet the passengers with a pitch for Elizabeth's home cooking at the hotel, saying, "If you don't get enough to eat, it won't cost you a dime."

The Brokaw House was famous for its dining room, which featured lace tablecloths and an elaborate Sunday menu of oyster stew, roast turkey, duck, roast beef, lamb, tongue salad, mashed potatoes, suet pudding, apple, mince, custard and blueberry pies, ice cream, and assorted cakes, all prepared by Elizabeth in a kitchen with an enormous woodburning stove, while her ingredients were kept fresh by great blocks of ice packed in wood shavings in an icehouse.

Somewhere along the way, a Roman Catholic priest converted Elizabeth and she became a devout Catholic, rejecting the Huguenot connection. Nine of her children followed suit, and to this day my cousins, aunts, and uncles on that side of the family are devout Catholics.

In the fall of 1912, William and Elizabeth were expecting their tenth child. That was my father, and somehow the Catholic priest missed him in the conversion crusade.

That's where this Brokaw prairie saga really begins.

CHAPTER 2

Anthony Orville Brokaw—
"Red"

ON OCTOBER 12, 1912, Elizabeth delivered a husky boy, more than twelve pounds, the carrot-top that would be so much a part of his identity already showing. This latest addition to the Brokaw family would soon shed his baptismal name and become known first as Snooks, after a newspaper cartoon character, and then, for most of his life, as Red.

Red came into the world as American politics was in turmoil. He was born during the presidency of William Howard Taft, a portly Ohio Republican who had the blessing of the outgoing president, the rambunctious Theodore "Teddy" Roosevelt.

Roosevelt, ever the contrarian, soon became unhappy with Taft and split from the Republican Party that had elected him president. Instead, T.R. ran as the nominee of his own invention, the Bull Moose Party. Woodrow Wilson, a scholar and former president of Princeton University, was the Democratic nominee, and when T.R. divided his own party, it opened the door for Wilson to be elected.

Wilson had an ambitious platform of reform including tariff, banking, and business changes that would diminish the power of Wall Street and big-money interests. However, his international ambitions and his deteriorating health, which his wife was determined to keep secret, in his second term seriously damaged his place in history.

In 1912 South Dakota went for Teddy Roosevelt, the Bull Moose. Later, another aristocratic Roosevelt, Franklin, a Democrat, won favor in South Dakota as the populist who led the country through the early days of the devastating Great Depression.

Through all that turmoil, national politics were not high on the agenda of the Brokaw family. Every day in Bristol was a struggle.

From the beginning, Red had a difficult life. His siblings treated him as their errand boy, assigning him the junkyard chores in the hotel, which was always in need of brute labor.

He also had what is now called a learning disability. Like other members of the family, he was born with hearing deficiencies, which affected his learning skills. He dropped out of school after the second grade.

At age six he strolled the early evening streets of Bristol advertising the upcoming motion pictures at the local theater. When he finished his movie advertisement chores, he'd often fall asleep in one of the theater seats, and the owner would simply lock up with Red still in the theater. Dad would wake up and stumble back to whatever hotel room was available.

The Brokaw House Hotel anchored one corner of Bristol's main street. Most big events in the small town began there: the Memorial Day parade, the annual dinner for the volunteer firemen, and the Fourth of July celebration.

The hotel was a lively but spartan establishment with hearty food, plain rooms, and toilets at the end of the hall. It was a smoky, noisy place, popular with itinerant railroad men and traveling salesmen, who

Brokaw House Hotel, Bristol, South Dakota

displayed their goods for the benefit of local merchants on long tables in a sample room just off the lobby.

The rooms were small and sparsely furnished, but they were clean, and the entire establishment had a homey feel. It was more like a large rooming house than a conventional hotel. Many of the guests were men, many with thick mustaches and large, gnarled hands.

Leona, the eldest Brokaw daughter, was the straw boss of the hotel, and all the Brokaw children worked there until they left for other occupations.

Dad's siblings became ranchers, a chef, workers in a Bristol creamery, a commercial salmon fisherman, a postal worker, and a Boy Scouts executive who also worked in a California post office. They were close as a family.

One of the hotel's patrons was Oscar Johnson, a Swedish immigrant who had come to America as a teenager and for a time homesteaded in what we call West River country, the grassland west of the Missouri River, which bisects the state.

The Homestead Act was initiated by President Abraham Lincoln to encourage further settlement in the vast areas of the American West. Applicants got 160 acres of free land if they "proved" it up in two years—that is, made it productive and settled on the land. It was a hard bargain. Much of the land was undeveloped prairie, short on rainfall and long on challenges, with thin topsoil and difficult access to markets.

**Railroad station in Bristol,
South Dakota, 1940**

My wife, Meredith, had a very tough great-grandmother who was paid fifty cents a day to occupy homestead claims in the same area where Oscar settled. She took her children in a covered wagon to the barren prairie and somehow kept her end of the deal through harsh winters and brutally hot, dry summers. I've not been able to find accounts of how she managed, but it must have been a daily trial in the open prairie, finding shelter, food, and some income.

As for Oscar, he stayed long enough in West River country to prove up his claim, which meant he now owned the land. With that, he moved to Bristol, in the northeastern corner of South Dakota, bought some cattle, and ran a one-man operation repairing and drilling new wells and fencing land.

Oscar moved into The Brokaw House and lived

there for fifty years, living in a single room with the bath down the hall. The lone light switch was next to the door, so he rigged up a long cord that he could operate from his bed.

Oscar would need an assistant, and Red Brokaw was a perfect fit. At the age of eight Dad went to work for Oscar, becoming, in effect, his foster son and right-hand man. They were the "go-to pair" of the prairie, on call to solve the toughest problems.

Red was already smoking by the age of ten, a habit he continued until he was fifty-five. His workaday life was more suited to someone twice his age, and it showed in his muscular physique. Farm kids would come to town to challenge the pugnacious redhead and invariably end up bloodied. He was aware he was often blamed for whatever went wrong in town, even though he was too busy working to get involved in mischief.

Red, toughest kid in town

Before long, local farmers who hired Oscar for country chores realized their chances of a job well done improved if Oscar brought along his redheaded hired hand. It was the beginning of an adventurous working-class life that lifted Red to heights he could not have imagined as a youngster working on difficult prairie projects.

When he was in his early fifties, Dad stunned us all by sitting down with a tape recorder and remembering the good times and the difficult.

Looking back, I think Red decided he was finally free of the short leash between financial anxiety and financial security. He was also quietly proud of his long marriage to Mother and their common values, their shared vision of how to raise a family and be a good citizen. Moreover, to a much greater degree than I realized, he had a keen memory of his early struggles just to survive. His emotional radar was finely tuned, and he learned early that only he could retool perceptions others had of him as a street tough with not many smarts.

The inner Red who emerged in the recordings surprised even those of us in the family who knew his early life had been difficult. We had no idea just how difficult it had been, and how much it had shaped him personally. He almost never invoked his childhood in raising my brothers and me.

That early life now looks like a twentieth-century Dark Age, and as I write this amid all the chaos of the twenty-first century, I think there are lessons to be learned and passed on.

His unspoken guide to life was never give up, never complain.

CHAPTER 3

The Brokaw House

I
N ITS GLORY DAYS, The Brokaw House Hotel was the center of the Day County universe. Community celebrations started and finished there. The lobby and dining room were seldom empty.

Everyone in the family had chores. Red and his brother Richard were just eight and ten when they were assigned to provide the firewood for the monstrous cookstove in the kitchen. The stove heated a fifty-gallon water container that had to be constantly monitored. It was a brutal task. The firewood was made up of discarded railroad ties, which had been soaked in creosote to preserve them and make them rock hard to saw through.

The brothers were also in charge of the coal supply that arrived by train from North Dakota. The great big chunks of coal each weighed a hundred pounds or more, and Dad and Rich would have to break them to force them into the stove. In the fall, they were responsible for organizing 125 pounds of potatoes to be stored in basement bins.

Once the stove was heated up and the water boiling, it was time for cooking. Red remembered seeing his brother Clarence and sister Leona carrying enormous trays of dishes into the dining room for Sunday dinners or a slightly reduced menu on weeknights. Clarence liked the choreography of serving, and Red wasn't surprised when his elder brother left Bristol and became a chef in North Dakota.

Red on a horse

After dinner, the patrons divided themselves into two groups. The ladies and children socialized in a parlor and the men next door in the hotel office, which was always thick with cigar smoke. Those were the Sunday meals, and the daily menu wasn't much lighter.

Dad remembered hearing his father rise at 4:00 A.M. to feed the working-class crowd—folks who were headed into the fields or onto the incoming trains. Red's mother was up an hour later for a full-blown breakfast. Her day started at 5:00 A.M. and didn't end until more than twelve hours later.

Her hard life as cook, hotel manager, and mother of ten caught up to her. She was forty-one when she died of cancer. She was so admired in Bristol that her funeral stopped all activity in town so residents could pay their respects.

Red, as the youngest of the brood, was especially close to his mother, and before he was even a teenager, he wondered what would happen to him when she was gone. His father, Bill, was not much help with the family or around the hotel, where he preferred to spend hours playing gin rummy. Bill Brokaw was also a bit of a drinker, and a part-time night cop. Apparently one of the small-town amusements was to stir up a dispute between the town's two cops and then watch them try to arrest each other. Red, who later kept his dad's service revolver in his top drawer, could not have been amused by those scenes. He mentioned them to me only once, laughing lightly.

When young Red shared his anxiety with his sister Ann about losing his mother, he was also suffering from the flu, and he remembered crying, wondering what would happen to him. Ann immediately said, "You deserve your own room." So a room was set aside for Red with a standard oak bureau, of which he claimed ownership by writing his initials in ink on the back side of the mirror. He was twelve years old.

Mother and Dad's first trip to New York to visit us was Dad's dream come true from the days when he was a boy in Bristol and stood on a stool to pretend he was on a skyscraper.

We had a spacious apartment, a long way from Red's hardscrabble boyhood, but it turned out there was a connection. As our youngest daughter, Sarah, showed him her bedroom, he thought an oak bureau looked familiar. He tipped it forward for a closer look and there was his long-ago handwritten signature: Anton Brokaw.

What a long way he had traveled.

Still, New York was intimidating. On a ride back from a visit to the Statue of Liberty, Dad was sitting across from Mother and me on the subway. Mother and I, typically, were chatting when the train came to what I thought was our stop. It wasn't, but Dad had already bolted off the subway and the doors were closing.

When he realized his mistake, he jammed his muscular arms into the narrow opening and began to reopen the mechanical door.

Other passengers were suddenly wide-eyed, and Mother said, quietly, "He's going to tip over the train."

He didn't, of course, and when he finally regained his seat he said, "This damn train wasn't leaving without me."

The other passengers joined us in laughing.

When we came to the right stop, this time Dad waited for me to make the first move.

CHAPTER 4

Oscar and Red

LIFE ON THE early-twentieth-century prairie was
defined by the physical labor that started early
every day and ended late. A ritual on workday mornings in Bristol involved the tall, gaunt Oscar on his
horse-drawn wagon with Red as they headed out to
the countryside for a job.

There were no federal or state rules on child labor
or worker safety at the time, and even if there had
been Oscar likely would have ignored them. Oscar
and his young assistant were in constant demand.

Red remembered one bitterly cold day when they
were putting in a new well for a farmer. They hooked
up an auger, a kind of drill, to a horse, which would
walk in a circle while the auger dug through the
earth. On those rocky plains this was a stop-and-go
proposition. As the hole deepened the auger would
often get hung up on a piece of glacial till, large rocks
left over from the Ice Age. Red would have a rope

attached to one leg and be dropped headfirst into the well to dislodge the rock.

Deeper and deeper, over and over, he would be lowered to wrestle loose the villain boulder. Hard, dirty work until the well's depth had been reached, and then he'd have to recover the rock and carry it in his arms as he was pulled out of the muddy hole.

He remembered one time finishing a hard assignment and changing out of his dirty clothes just as a small piglet being chased by a dog tumbled into the deep well shaft. Red changed back into his dirty clothes and once again was lowered forty feet. As he recalled, "If you don't think that's hard, one leg with a rope around it, imagine trying to hang on to a squealing pig as they hauled me up." All in a day's work for a redheaded tough kid.

Windmills were essential to the open-prairie farm families. The water supply was stored in shallow depths in the soil and rock layers of this semi-arid land where winters were arctic and summers Saharan. The windmills were subject to damage from their constant battering by high winds. As I grew up on that prairie, just writing that sentence immediately brought back memories of walking to school backward against the unrelenting wind or just leaning at a 45-degree angle going forward.

In recordings Red made toward the end of his life, he shared a harrowing account of trying to shut down a runaway windmill on a windy day. "The brake on the windmill was broken, so they couldn't shut off the whirling blades. The wind was blowing real hard so I had to climb up onto a platform that was only about two feet square. I had to crawl on the back side of the wheel while it was spinning madly, crawl up over the platform, get one hand on the whirring windmill, the other on the tail fifty feet in the air—and push it around until I could get it into the wind. Then get a rope over the wheel to hold it in place while I installed new gears. No safety ropes while I stood way up there in the howling wind."

Often when that job was done, he'd prepare for the job of mowing the high prairie grass behind a team of big horses. As he recalled, "I was too short to rig them both at once, so I'd tilt the rigging to one side to hook up one horse and then repeat the procedure on the other." Oscar would put a wood block on the foot brace so Red could get up, and off they'd go. "If I had fallen off, I would have been caught in the mowing spindles." Sixty years later he agreed. "It was quite dangerous for a kid at nine or ten."

My maternal great-grandfather, Tom Conley, farmed a thousand acres south of Bristol with just the help of his wife. It was all horse-drawn equipment.

On the Fourth of July he'd pick up my grandfather nearby, shouting, "Hurray for the Fourth of July! Let's go to the lake." The next day he'd be back in the fields. That was Tom and Matilda Conley's holiday for the year.

CHAPTER 5

Winter Journeys and Hard Days

IN THE EVENING when young Red's kitchen chores were finished and other kids his age were in the streets of Bristol playing before bedtime, he still had chores to do in the barn. "My jobs weren't finished until the cows were milked and the horses fed."

Even then, the night would beckon with other jobs. He recalled a cold winter night when he was about ten and his brother Richard maybe twelve, and their job was to drive two teams of horses to Webster, which was thirteen miles away, and move a large building back to Bristol.

They got to Webster and jacked the building onto timbers fifty feet long and twelve by twelve inches. The wooden sled was attached to iron wheels three feet high that Oscar had salvaged from a grain separator. Between them the brothers had four horses and thirteen miles to go. It was below freezing.

Red remembered hearing the Webster fire whistle signaling 6:00 P.M. as they left. They arrived back in Bristol six hours later, cold and tired, but before bed they had to unleash the horses and get them into the barn. Then they raced to an empty, unheated bedroom just above the kitchen, so cold they could see their breath in the frigid air. They jumped into bed fully clothed and covered up with what blankets they could find and a buffalo robe left over from Oscar's days as a homesteader.

A few years later, Rich left Bristol for California and enlisted first in the Coast Guard, and then in the Navy during World War II. Red was on his own then as Oscar's only hired hand, drilling more wells and moving more

Red with sisters Celia and Ann

buildings. One building was dropped at the head of Main Street and stayed there for sixty years.

Curiously, Dad never mentioned the great 1918 flu pandemic that ripped through America. In one year in the sparsely populated state, 1,847 South Dakotans died of the flu. In contrast to the current South Dakota governor's hands-off attitude regarding precautionary measures, the state's 1918 governor shut down most of the businesses. In villages and larger towns, sporting events, schools, social occasions, and funerals were canceled or tightly controlled. People were told to stay off the streets.

Meredith's grandmother Edith lived in cowboy country and rode horseback from ranch to ranch to help families as best she could without becoming a victim of the flu herself.

The epidemic was over by the time Red was approaching his teens.

One of Red's most vivid memories was the Bristol celebration of the end of World War I. He recalled a big bonfire and a hanging in effigy of Kaiser Wilhelm, the German emperor who led his country into a disastrous war. Even though the South Dakota countryside was laced with German settlers, the main street was lit by a big bonfire and fireworks.

In less than twenty years, the United States would again be at war with Germany, this time in historic proportions, and local German American families, many of whom had relatives still in the motherland, were emotionally distraught.

As for Red, although he was still a school dropout, many of his weekends were spent with pals his age who had normal family lives. One weekend the boys were riding in the country when a billowing prairie storm blew up. The host mother called parents to say the kids should spend the night on her farm. She looked at Dad and said, "I don't have to call the hotel because they don't care where you are."

She was a strict Lutheran and wanted to know about his church attendance. He said, "The closest I get to your church on Sundays is when I herd the cows out to pasture." He could tell from her reaction that she was appalled, so he quietly decided to become the town Good Samaritan. He delivered milk to widows for half price, ran errands for the penniless barber, and helped others with a variety of chores.

He did have limits. He was maybe fourteen when he delivered a supply of coal to the town banker. When he finished shoveling the delivery into the basement, he spread a light layer of snow on the coal to keep the dust down. The banker came storming out of his house, shouting that he didn't want snow on his coal. Dad did him one better. He shoveled the entire load of his delivery back into his wagon and told the banker to get his winter supply elsewhere.

CHAPTER 6

A Pair
of Sorrels

WITH HIS MOTHER GONE and his brother Rich off to California and the Coast Guard, Red was more alone than ever. Then one day his fortune changed and set him on a track for the rest of his life. At a horse sale he spotted a pair of matching sorrel colts, a sturdy and popular breed. It was love at first sight. Oscar negotiated a price of forty dollars for the pair, and Dad worked out a long-term loan with Oscar.

As he remembered more than fifty years later, "I loved that pair more than anything else in the world. I decorated their harnesses, and we went to work. I hauled five hundred gallons of soft water for a dollar. I got forty cents for a ton of coal. Twenty cents for loading it and twenty cents for delivering it. I had customers all over town. In the spring we'd plow gardens and run errands."

As a teenager Red was doing the work of a grown man seven days a week. Two of his best friends, local athletes, told me later they tried to recruit him for Sunday baseball games, but he never had time. That was true for the rest of his life too. Work in one form or another was his calling seven days a week.

Reflecting on his teenage years, Dad said, "I didn't take time off. There was always a field to be plowed or hay to be cut. I never owned a bicycle. It was just hard work all the time." That was not a self-pitying observation. It was a matter-of-fact summary for many young men at that time. Many country boys stopped their education in the eighth grade.

It's clear Dad was keenly aware of his deprivations, but he didn't dwell on them. The toughest kid in town privately knew he was in a family where it was every man and woman struggling to survive.

If there was a buck to be made, Red could find a way to get involved. He became a member of a roller-skating troupe called the Dakota Ramblers. They'd travel through northern South Dakota doing roller-skating choreography at local fairs and church outings. It was typical of Red. He'd "play" if he got paid for it.

Motorcycle hill climbs were also a big attraction, and they paid a small purse. In his first outing Red lost control about halfway up and was thrown from the bike, which continued to spin around until he got it shut down. He learned a lesson, and by the end of the day he was the champion.

He became a regular on the circuit and rode his bike for transportation around Bristol. He would get involved in races and climbs only if there was a cash payoff. That was his attitude toward recreation. If it pays, okay. If not, I'll find something else to do.

It didn't always work the way he hoped. During the Depression, America was filled with men looking for a payday. One such man passed through Bristol, a professional boxer from Minneapolis, a traveling pugilist seeking action. Dad's buddies in Bristol nominated him, saying he was the toughest guy in town. Red showed up, a small-town brawler against the traveling pro. It was over in a hurry. Dad was knocked out in the first round and never talked about it, but his buddies made sure I knew. I decided not to ask Dad for details.

When Dad became a father to three boys, other fathers played baseball or fished with their sons. Dad's lifelong idea of recreation was adding a bedroom and a bathroom in the basement or converting the underpinning of an older car into a framework for a trailer. We didn't object, because his preference for working alone allowed us to pursue our interests.

One time, he did ask me to weed Mother and Dad's bountiful garden of tomatoes, strawberries, cucumbers, corn, and potatoes. I did a fast job because I was late for a baseball game. When I returned, he said, "Okay, time to get to the garden." When I started to protest, he said, "Mr. Browne so appreciated your help, because it was **his** garden you weeded.

"Now it's my turn." Smile.

Dad rarely took time for recreation, so my brothers

and I tried to persuade him to go swimming with us at a popular lake with an enclosed swimming section. He showed up with an aged bathing suit, a sunburn from his neck to his hairline and the rest of his body alabaster white due to his redhead genes.

When we arrived at the swimming section, a large crowd was gathered around a shocking sight. A husky male swimmer was totally inert as a local lifeguard was desperately trying to breathe life into him. It was futile. The victim, a construction worker, had broken his neck on a dive into a shallow section. We got back into our car and went home.

Dad never did go swimming with us, but when Meredith and I had three daughters we took them to Evans Plunge, a celebrated hot springs pool in the Black Hills of South Dakota. They were having a jolly time when suddenly I saw a familiar red head in their midst.

It was Dad, now in his sixties, the first time I ever saw him in a pool. Jennifer, Andrea, and Sarah were whooping it up with their red-haired grandfather. I laughed and cried some, thinking of how life had changed for the kid from the hotel.

CHAPTER 7

A Perfect Match—Man and Machine

THE BIG CHANGE FOR RED as a young man in Bristol came when he had gained a reputation as an eager worker willing to take on all tasks with his team of sorrel horses. When highway construction teams showed up in Bristol to extend and improve the highway running alongside the rail line, Red and his horse team were hired to help shape the embankments.

At first the contractor wanted to hire only Red's team. Red said, "No, I'd have to be part of the deal." They settled on terms. Red and his horse team were hired for forty cents an hour, with Red in charge. In his town work the max he could expect was a dollar a day.

His life was about to change in yet another way that he could not have anticipated at the time. The construction crew had a Caterpillar road grader parked nearby and no one equipped to run it. Dad had a friend who had operated one the summer before who volunteered to be his instructor.

Red on a "Cat"

It was the beginning of a lifelong match of man and machine. Before long, with Dad at the gears, the Caterpillar was making complicated turns with grace and efficiency. The contractor kept Red busy with big Cat earth-moving jobs and the ancillary work of removing trees, clearing brush, and sloping the banks. He became a one-man operator with his horse team and new Cat skills: chopping down trees, clearing brush, and then mounting the Cat for the heavy work of shaping the emerging highway.

Red obviously made a big impression, because the contractor hired him at the end of the summer to drive the Cat back to a Minnesota site 150 miles away. That meant back roads at a turtle's pace and a steady roar from the diesel engine. It took Red four days of navigating, sleeping in barns, and losing more hearing. The contractor promised him a job as soon as the Midwestern weather cleared in spring.

Back in Bristol, Red's role was changing. He was no longer the tough little roughneck. Girls started to notice, and Red suddenly had a social life and access to the local barber's car. He now had social standing to go with his handsome stature and striking red hair.

CHAPTER 8

The Conleys

R ED CONTINUED TO WORK FOR OSCAR, and as he recalled, laughing, "It wasn't all work for the old Swede. Oscar never worked on the Fourth of July!

"One farmer came up to us on a Fourth of July and said his well needed repairing because a critical part had worn out. 'If you'll help me,' he said, 'my wife will make you the best Fourth of July dinner you've ever had.'"

More than fifty years later, Dad remembered the dinner, as the midday meal was called. It was fuel for the hard work still ahead. "Fried chicken, mashed potatoes and gravy, and strawberry shortcake with real whipped cream three inches thick." It was not unusual for those old-timers to take off just one day a year—the Fourth of July or Christmas.

South of Bristol, Dad's future was on a county road of farms occupied by German, Swedish, and Norwegian families, and a particular Irish family, the Conleys. The farms were conventional for the times—mostly corn, a few cows, hogs, chickens, and a couple of workhorses. Farming results were at best uneven. Following World War I, agriculture across the country went into a steep dive.

It recovered by the mid-1920s, when farmers began to organize into collectives that improved their negotiating power, but a historic disaster was coming on fast. Herbert Hoover, an Iowan who had gained international fame for organizing relief for Europe following World War I, was elected president and immediately put a barrier around the American economy, in the form of high tariffs on U.S. goods, in the mistaken belief that that would protect American producers.

It was a disastrous decision. The high tariffs drove off foreign investors just as the American stock market collapsed in a binge of reckless speculation and the agricultural regions were hit by a historic drought.

The largest farm in the Bristol area, occupying a thousand acres, was owned by Tom Conley, a former railroad man who had moved to the Dakota territory to raise four sons and a stay-at-home daughter. The second son was Jim Conley, small but athletic and a good-time Irishman. Their father insisted on college educations for the boys. The eldest became a prominent Minneapolis lawyer. Jim was a pharmacist. A third brother was in the Navy during World War I and returned home to become a local ladies' man. The fourth brother was a physician and lived in an Iowa community for half a century.

Jim Conley gave up his pharmacist career in Minneapolis, returned to South Dakota, and set out to farm 120 debt-laden acres next to his father's much larger spread. He had come home to South Dakota with a pharmacy degree and a wife, Ethel Baker, a handsome, lively city girl from a prosperous middle-class family.

Ethel arrived in South Dakota in 1917 with a newborn—my mother, Eugenia Baker Conley—and no farm experience. She had left a leafy Minneapolis neighborhood for the bar-ren South Dakota prairie. When she arrived on a treeless prairie as a newly-wed, Ethel's first home was a railroad car, and then they moved to a half-finished small house. A rudimentary lower floor combined sleeping quar-ters and a small living room. The kitchen was mostly a giant stove called the Majestic. It served as an oven, an incubator for newborn chicks, and a place to cook stove-top meals.

Jim and Ethel just before the Depression, 1927

What Grandma Ethel brought to this new life was a lively sense of humor and a willingness to learn. She planted a big garden and raised rabbits and chickens to trade in town for store-bought goods. She also learned to cook the hearty meals of farm life, where dinner is the heavy noontime meal for working-class fuel. Supper is the evening meal, another energy-packed menu of stews, fried chicken, pork dishes, and bread, always a lot of bread. A late-night snack is called lunch.

Ethel, with her sparkling personality, fit right in with other farm families who often worked together to survive.

Mother remembered a local farmer famous for his ingenuity. He'd have a party, inviting neighbors to an evening of making rope on a spindle stretching across his kitchen. The women would bake, catch up on knitting, and gossip. Mother said the evening would end with a potluck supper and dancing.

In the early 1920s, during her first years on the farm, Ethel would occasionally get homesick for her family and the city attractions of Minneapolis. Grandpa Jim would arrive from a day in the fields in the late afternoon to find Ethel with her bag packed, ready to catch the Milwaukee Road evening train to the Twin Cities. He didn't try to talk her out of a rejuvenating trip home. He knew this prairie life was so much more difficult than the middle-class city life she had left behind.

My mother began life on that lonely landscape. She remembered doing her homework by pulling up a chair to the opened door of the Majestic stove and studying in the reflected heat.

We can only imagine what Ethel's father thought when he visited from Minneapolis, where he had a good-paying job as a supervisor in one of the General Mills operations. Mother remembered her grand-father taking long walks across the prairie, no doubt wondering what his lively city daughter had got-ten herself into. Before he boarded the train back to the city, he'd tuck some cash into Ethel's hand, and once he was gone, she'd go with Jim to Aberdeen to spend it.

A big prize was a rudimentary low voltage radio that could draw in broadcasts from Pittsburgh. Grandpa Jim would stay up late listening through earphones to far-off news and sporting events. When morning came, he'd have to face the reality of a strug-gling farm, a drought, and a collapsing economy.

There was something else. It wasn't until my mother, Jean, was in her seventies that I saw a copy of her birth certificate and realized Grandma Ethel had been pregnant with Jean when she and Jim were married. What's more, Jim had lured her away from his brother, the prominent lawyer, who

Jean, age two

never again talked to Jim or Ethel. When I made my discovery, I asked how many people were aware. Mother said almost no one. She did the math when she was seven or eight and kept the secret.

Mother's recollections of her days on the farm had that Little House on the Prairie quality made familiar by Laura Ingalls Wilder, whose family lived on a farm eighty miles south of Bristol.

When she was not a city girl, but a farmer's wife, Ethel's days were filled with hard labor. Washdays involved manipulating a wooden washer by hand as the clothes were boiled and rinsed in several waters, then hung on the line to dry. In winter, the wet wash would freeze and have to be carried into the house stiff, then thawed. Wash water would be saved to scrub the outdoor toilet. Churning butter was another tough weekly chore.

Mother on the farm with her cousin Muriel

Mother from an early age was part of the farm labor, and in her memoirs, she seemed to enjoy it. She drove a team of horses and managed her part of the garden. It was, after all, what all other young girls were doing on nearby farms.

Mother was especially close to her father, my Grandpa Jim, even though he treated childhood illnesses with castor oil or, drawing on his pharmacy training, a home brew of other over-the-counter elixirs. It must have worked, because by the age of thirteen Mother was declared the healthiest girl in the county by a touring nurse.

During the school year, Mother walked more than a mile down a country road to a one-room schoolhouse, which served grades one through eight. She carried her lunch in an empty Karo syrup can with her initials punched into the lid. She was bright and outgoing, so she was skipped a grade by her

Mother, age fifteen

teachers, who called on her to help with the lower grades as she grew older. Later, she put the romantic image of a one-room school into perspective. "Teachers were often there for only one year," she said. "It was mostly the fundamentals—reading, writing, and arithmetic. No science classes, or expansive history studies."

So, when her mother took those train trips home

to the big city of Minneapolis, Ethel was retreating to a far different life than the one she was living on the barren prairie. She would be back in a week, ready to resume the spartan farm life, helped, no doubt, by the company of her neighbors. After a year or two the trips home came to an end and her place among the Swedes, Norwegians, and Germans was secure.

But dark days were moving in. Everyone was already struggling to make a success out of this challenging land and weather, as well as the economic challenges that came with the protective tariffs imposed by President Herbert Hoover. It was a historic and calamitous miscalculation by Hoover.

The higher tariffs that were supposed to protect American producers instead sent buyers to more affordable markets. All this happened just as the rain dried up, just as desperate farmers tried to expand their output by plowing more ground—going deep to stir up the topsoil, which ignited ferocious dust storms in a land short on rain.

Farm income in South Dakota dropped precipitously. In 1925 South Dakota farmland had been worth $44.89 an acre. It began its collapse in 1930, and by 1938 it was worth only $17.00 an acre and was not recovering. Mother remembered her father staring into the west at daybreak, hoping for rains that rarely came. One year he produced a bumper crop of corn that brought only a dollar a bushel. A year later, corn dropped even more, to a penny a bushel. He fed his corn to the hogs. It was not worth the effort to take his crop to market.

Jim Conley was caught in the twin pincers of the economy and the ferocious turn of nature to hot, dry winds and epic swarms of manic grasshoppers. Jean Conley's Little House on the Prairie life was coming to an end. She had grown up riding behind her father and his team of horses as he pointed out constellations in the nighttime sky.

Grandpa had been a Republican until Herbert Hoover from next-door Iowa introduced his disastrous policies. Jim Conley reregistered as a Democrat and voted for Franklin Delano Roosevelt, who became the family political hero. Hoover was an Iowa farm boy with a Stanford degree and Roosevelt a wealthy aristocrat, yet as presidents their policies were contrary to their upbringings.

Years later, historians interviewed Midwestern farmers who described dust storms so ferocious their well-constructed homes were swamped by layers of prairie dirt at the end of the day. Other farmers remembered grasshoppers coming in such vicious swarms they would invade a house and eat through cupboards, furniture, beds, and clothing within an hour.

The American political scene was roiling, not just because of the weather, but also because of the prairie's strong resistance to distant, powerful, big-city financial institutions that controlled so much of the economy.

South Dakota, which is now such a bastion of free enterprise, in those days established state-owned gas stations and a state-owned quarry to control the costs of necessities in the local economy. Mother remembered her father attending a meeting of a populist organization—she wasn't sure which one. Several were organized to collectively take on large agricultural companies that controlled the markets. Mother said Grandfather came home, saying it wasn't for him. My guess is that it was too radical for his lingering Republican inclinations. He decided to go it alone.

Grandpa Jim knew the bank was closing in and foreclosure on his farm was imminent. He desperately wanted a new heifer calf to take with them when they left the farm so at least they'd have a milk supply. It took several tries, but as time was running out, a heifer was produced to go with them to a small rental home with room for a garden in Andover, fifteen miles to the west. Mother transferred to Andover High School for her final year and was forced to give up her goal of studying journalism at Northern State Teachers College in nearby Aberdeen.

Her father went to work for a friend, the enterprising German émigré John Hansmeier, who was introducing alfalfa to the prairie and buying up distressed farmland to expand his holdings. Jim Conley was paid ten cents an hour and his lunch. At the end of his shift he'd call on other farming families and peddle household goods such as needles and thread, first-aid items, and toiletries. When he'd return home he

**The Dust Bowl in Dallas,
South Dakota, 1936**

would tell Ethel, "There are people out there worse off than us."

However, he was a beaten man. There had been stories about his mischievous childhood and busy social calendar while he was studying to be a pharmacist in Minneapolis. Now he was a quiet, somber soul, while Grandma Ethel retained her lively ways. Her large garden in Andover helped feed the family and brought in badly needed cash at the local markets.

The farming life in that part of America had been problematic since the crash following World War I. In the mid-twenties, agriculture began to recover with the help of cooperatives formed to give farmers unified strength in the marketplace. But there were other deadly practices at work in the dark fallout from the historic stock-market crash of October 1929 that set off ten years of struggles in the American economy. In the first ten months of 1930 more than seven hundred banks failed, mostly in the Midwest. North and South Dakota lost 150,000 residents to states they hoped would provide a more promising future.

As the banking crisis spread, some banks declared holidays—temporary shutdowns aimed at keeping the banks solvent by not requiring them to meet withdrawal demands.

In 1932 the country turned to Franklin Delano Roosevelt, an aristocrat with a common man's heart. He came to office promising a New Deal for the American people. A public works program was started to build parks, highways, bridges, and other infrastructure needs, but even though three million jobs were created it was not enough to handle the desperate need for income.

CHAPTER 9

Courtship, the Depression, and World War II

At about the same time, Red Brokaw experienced a life-changing evening. He went to a Bristol school play in which the lead was Jean Conley. Even though she lived just south of Bristol, Red had never met her. He was no longer the scruffy school dropout, the hotel kid. Now he was winning more admirers for his hard work with his Caterpillar skills, his sorrel team, and his Good Samaritan ways with local residents who needed assistance.

Red's life changed that night when he went to the school play starring Mother in the lead role. He was instantly smitten. A friend encouraged him to ask her out.

In a story that became a family favorite, Red drove to the Conley farm and left his car running, with the doors open and the lights on. As he recalled later, when Jean came to the door, he stuttered and stammered asking if she'd like to see a movie. She turned to her dad, who said, "It's okay. He has a good reputation as a hard worker." Before long they were a couple.

In the early stages of their relationship, Jean and Red would often pile into a car with friends to see movies in the bigger town of Aberdeen. In the Depression, movie theaters would give free dishes to paying patrons, so the Bristol crowd would see one movie for dishes, another for drinking glasses. Those were the days when movie stars such as Henry Fonda, Clark Gable, Roz Russell, Kate Hepburn, Jimmy Stewart, Humphrey Bogart, and other marquee names were cinematic gods.

In California I came to know Henry Fonda, and years later, when his health was failing, Mother wrote him a letter. It was a note of gratitude, telling him how much he had meant to her and her friends during those difficult days. She sent it to his studio, and somehow it got to him. I know that because Hank's wife shared the letter with me, saying how much he had appreciated Mother's thoughtful note. When I asked Mother why she didn't enlist my help, she said it was **her** letter to someone she considered an old friend.

During their dating days, Mother and Dad were always in a car crowded with several couples, but one night they were alone as Red drove her home. They had never been alone before, and Mother remembered they were both speechless for a time. (She didn't say who talked first, but in our family we all put our money on Mom.)

That generation of prairie Midwesterners was accustomed to hard times, and they had little hope that their lives would get better anytime soon. They had watched from afar the giddy and ultimately disastrous collapse of Wall Street and the American economy. In 1929, with Wall Street at its wildly irresponsible peak, national unemployment was 3.2 percent. After the market crash and the roiling effect of droughts and bankruptcies across the American economy, in 1934 national unemployment was 21.7 percent. More than a fifth of the workforce was unemployed despite the government work programs initiated by President Roosevelt. The Dirty Thirties stretched on.

After high school, with no hope of attending college, Mother got a job as a waitress and another as a part-time clerk at the post office. The postmaster always used the same line as he paid her. "There you go, Jeannie. A dollar a day and in a million days you'll be a millionaire."

Red was busy on Midwestern construction projects, where his bosses kept him at the gears of the Caterpillar for as long as he would stay. On one job his boss called him over to clear out the excess dirt around a drainage pipe.

Red said, "You mean all three?"

His boss said, "It's time to take a break."

The Brokaw family, 1939.
Red and Jean are at far left,
arms linked.

There was only one pipe where Red had seen three. They added up his time, and he'd been operating the Cat for thirty-six hours with food delivered to him while he stayed at the gears.

At the end of a long shift, he'd make his way to Minneapolis to collapse for a twelve-hour sleep that could not be disturbed even though his room was directly above a Bohemian dance hall.

Mother had moved to Minneapolis and was staying with an aunt and uncle while working for Fanny Farmer, the well-known Twin Cities candy-store chain. Red's visits were irregular, and she had no other friends, so she returned to South Dakota.

Red was not far behind. In 1937 he drove from Minnesota to the Conley home in Andover and asked, "Do you want to get married?" It turns out Mother had already bought a sensible wedding dress and had lined up a minister in Andover. Red bought a new suit and got a haircut. Their honeymoon was one night in nearby Aberdeen.

The next day they were back in Red's Ford, heading to Minnesota where he had work waiting. They bought a small trailer and made a vow: They'd save a thousand dollars cash a year on Red's salary of fifty dollars a week for the ten months a year he worked. Midwestern winters were hard on outdoor construction.

As Americans struggled to deal with the devastating reality of the Depression, the dark news from Europe played out on the radio and in movie theaters. The Third Reich had occupied most of Europe and was determined to conquer Great Britain.

In the Pacific, Japan was spending 23 percent of its gross national product on military development. Germany, which had been building its military spending longer and had leftover armaments from World War I, was spending 13.5 percent. The United States? Just 1.39 percent of its GDP went for military expansion.

President Roosevelt continued to keep America out of harm's way politically, but he was preparing for the increasing possibility that the United

States, in one form or another, would have to get involved. He developed an ingenious plan to assist Great Britain. It was called Lend-Lease. The United States would lend or lease to Great Britain the armaments it needed to fight Germany without committing American troops to battle. That was a clever but controversial way of helping an ally without putting boots on the ground or pilots in the air. In the Pacific the Japanese were expanding their voracious appetite for critical territory.

The American economy was still struggling, and President Roosevelt's polls plummeted. Charles Lindbergh, the Minnesota aviator famous for his solo flight from Long Island to Paris, became an outspoken opponent of committing America to war against Germany or Japan. He made several trips to Germany and was treated like a visiting oracle. Lindbergh was in his own way as famous as President Roosevelt and therefore a formidable opponent.

FDR also wondered whether he could win reelection against a Republican newcomer from Indiana, Wendell Willkie. The U.S. economy remained stalled. Nonetheless FDR decided to run for an unprecedented third term, concerned that isolationists would keep America from confronting what was a growing threat from abroad.

Meanwhile Mother and Dad were starting a family. I was born on Grandpa Conley's birthday, February 6, 1940, into a world with Europe aflame in war, Japan preparing for war, and in too much of the

The Brokaw family

United States, deniers wanted no part of it, believing we were protected by two oceans, east and west. President Roosevelt was on a losing streak. He lost his ill-conceived attempt to pack the Supreme Court with additional, supportive justices and the economy was stalled at best. Later, when I asked Mother about the danger of war, she said they were so preoccupied with just making ends meet that the prospect of war seemed distant.

On December 7, 1941, the world changed. War came to America in a devastating surprise attack. Japan rained terror on the American ships, air bases, and guns at Pearl Harbor, Hawaii. More than 2,400 Americans were killed that day. The U.S. Pacific Fleet had been stacked up like sitting ducks in Pearl

Harbor. Twenty-one American ships, from small craft to battleships, were damaged or destroyed. America's illusion of being an untouchable fortress was over. It was, as President Roosevelt memorably proclaimed, "a date which will live in infamy."

The war instantly became, in every sense of the phrase, a world war unlike any other before or since. In London, the British prime minister Winston Churchill was privately elated. He now had the most powerful ally in the world at his side. America needed to become a world military power overnight, led by an aristocrat with a severe physical disability from polio.

The legendary **Washington Post** editor Ben Bradlee was a Harvard student in 1941, and he remembered being stunned when he walked into a Boston rail yard where Roosevelt was being loaded into a waiting car. Ben never forgot the scene. "My god," he told me, "it took a half a dozen men to get the president into his limousine, and he seemed to have little control of his body." But once propped up onstage or behind the wheel of a convertible with hand gears, he was a model of confidence and good cheer, ready to lead his country into war. When FDR died before the war was over and news accounts included his struggle with polio, many Americans realized for the first time the full extent of his physical limitations.

The day after Pearl Harbor, recruiting offices were

overrun with volunteers, including more than a few who just a few weeks earlier had been opposed to America going to war in foreign lands far away. Within a year, more than a million men and women were in uniform across the military branches, and that was just the beginning. City kids and farmers, doctors and schoolteachers, bankers and truck drivers, scientists, women and men signed up.

Posters with a determined Uncle Sam saying "I Want You!" were everywhere. But the shameful fact was that Negroes, as African Americans were then called, were mostly relegated to noncombatant roles as kitchen stewards or to stateside construction duty. Those who were involved in combat performed heroically.

It wasn't until late in the twentieth century that an African American who had been raised as a typical Wyoming teenager, hunting and fishing while his grandfather worked on the railroad, was belatedly awarded the Medal of Honor. Vernon Baker had led an all-Black unit on an assault against a German fortress in the mountainous north of Italy. His white commander had abandoned his post, but Baker continued the assault under heavy fire.

His unit found and destroyed German communications lines before engaging in a fierce firefight, immobilizing the German fortress. Nineteen of Baker's men were killed, but he continued his personal assault, killing at least nine enemy at close range. When he returned to his American base with a handful of bloody dog tags from his outfit's losses, a Southern Army officer gave him hell for not wearing his helmet.

When we met in 2004, Vernon had been belatedly awarded the Medal of Honor in a White House ceremony and was living in the mountains of Idaho, where he still hunted wild game. He was a congenial and modest man who was surprised but pleased by the Medal of Honor.

Outrageous discrimination also landed on America's sizable population of Japanese Americans, who lived mostly on the West Coast as successful merchants, fishermen, physicians, and pillars of their communities. On orders from President Roosevelt, they were forced to give up their homes and businesses as they were rounded up and shipped to spartan internment camps in the Mountain West or the desert.

In the foothills of the mountains surrounding Cody, Wyoming, the camp included several young Japanese men who actually received draft notices and were ordered to report for military duty. One of those who received the order said he'd report only if his aging parents were released. Army officials denied his request, and when he refused to report he was jailed. When his jail term was up, he left the compound and went to a nearby enlistment office to join the Army.

Some of the camps have been restored by succeeding generations of Japanese Americans who have created annual programs to honor their ancestors. These camps serve as a reminder of a shameful time in American history.

CHAPTER 10

The Black Hills Ordnance Depot

IGLOO, SOUTH DAKOTA.

During the early stages of World War II, America was in a rush to catch up at home and abroad, and Mother and Dad were on the move again. Red was sent to Kansas for the coldest winter he could remember, as he operated an open-cockpit Caterpillar in the middle of the wide-open spaces, home to new military air bases.

From Kansas, it was back to Minnesota, where Mother and Dad encamped near a small arms factory in New Brighton that was being converted from sporting guns to military weapons. It was a stop that gave the family an enduring phrase. When the landlady's son came home from six weeks of basic training, he walked into the house, looked around, and said, "Well, I see you have the same old cat." The phrase stayed in our family. As time went by, Mother would serve the same dish once too often and one of us would murmur, "Same old cat."

With the war under way, every family had new realities to consider. Mother and Dad knew of a military base where bombs, artillery shells, land mines, and other explosives were being rushed to safer territory. It was in the arid southwest corner of South Dakota, a sizable stretch of sagebrush and ancient red rock with just a few ranchers and sheep-herders.

Dad loaded up the 1939 Ford with the family, which now included my baby brother, Bill, and headed for the Black Hills

Dad's Army base badge

Ordnance Depot, commonly known as Igloo, where compounds made of earth held a variety of explosives. We were flatlanders in new territory: the legendary Black Hills of South Dakota, sacred ground to Native American people, who called the hills Paha Sapa. The mountain range also included Deadwood, the nineteenth-century gold-rush town famous for Calamity Jane and Wild Bill Hickok.

We drove through the night to get to the destination in the remote southern Black Hills, which were alive with wildlife. Bison and deer crossed the highway; a mountain lion loped alongside for a while, our headlights apparently an attraction. For this prairie family it was a wide-eyed experience. At daybreak it was a different reality. Igloo, as the base was called for the prairie dugouts where bombs, artillery, and mortar shells were stored, was a work in progress when we arrived.

Red was so dismayed by the barren surroundings that he wanted to turn around, but Mother prevailed, and so we settled into a tiny house—250 square feet—along with an assortment of civilian neighbors drawn by the chance for a decent wage after ten years of the Depression. In short order, Igloo became a functioning town with a rail line, hospital, shopping center, movie theater, post office, schools, and recreation center.

One neighborhood was filled with members of the surrounding Sioux tribes. Many of the Sioux who moved in stayed long enough for their children to graduate from high school. Later, several of them commented on what a rewarding experience living at Igloo had been.

The base was active twenty-four hours a day, with ordnance being tested in the prairie and U.S. troops performing their parade-ground drills. An unusual population was assigned to garbage details, snow removal, and grounds maintenance; they were Italian prisoners of war who had been shipped over from the war zone for security and to work as labor on American bases.

They wore bright orange coveralls and were a constant presence on the base. They'd chat among themselves in their native language and were generally a cheerful presence. When I was older, Mother told me they were also active in other ways. She said it was well known that a number of them had affairs with homebound American wives whose husbands were overseas, many of them fighting relatives of the Igloo Italians.

Other women on the base had new roles to fill. One of my fixed memories is of a big Army truck—an eight-wheeler—stopping in front of our house and the driver popping out to check the cargo. It was a woman in a red bandanna, overalls, and boots. When she finished her inspection, she swung back into the cab and pulled away.

Grandpa and Grandma Conley followed us to Igloo and Jim got a job that reflected his professional decline. He was a night superintendent at the sewage plant. However, the war was his passion. He followed the tides of battle through radio, **Time** magazine, and the newsreels in movie theaters. Battlefields on land, at sea, in the air—on all the continents—were filled with epic stories of heroism, death, and a world forever changed.

Dad kept Mother's picture on his watch.

It is impossible to single out a representative story of World War II, but for me, when I later became involved in documenting the war, one ordinary American became a lodestar. I met him on the fortieth anniversary of D Day, when a new generation of Americans was developing a full appreciation of the challenges, sacrifices, and roles of ordinary Americans thrown into the greatest war in history.

Gino Merli found himself in the thick of a German assault on American positions in Belgium during the Battle of the Bulge, when Hitler made a desperate attempt to break the American forces trapped in a Nazi pincer assault. Merli volunteered to cover a nighttime retreat by his outfit. In one long night Merli killed more than forty enemy attackers. When a new wave of Germans attacked, he'd collapse into the foxhole, faking his death next to his already dead partner until the Germans swept by, and then he would rise to attack them.

When daylight came, he was rescued, and he asked to be taken to a nearby church so he could pray for a gravely wounded German soldier he heard moaning through the night outside his foxhole. He could hear the German apparently trying to alert onrushing Nazis that Merli was alive and lethal. Merli later was awarded the Medal of Honor and spent his civilian years as a New Jersey sheriff's deputy.

After six long years of the war, the best estimates were that more than sixty million combatants and civilians had been killed in history's greatest war. Nations, cultures, economies, would never be the same.

When he was thirty-two, Dad's draft number came up for active duty. He reported to the Denver induction office, hoping to be assigned to an outfit that could utilize his heavy-equipment skills in developing landing zones and for battlefield clearances. But before Dad had finished his physical, his Igloo base commander called the Denver office and requested that he defer Red Brokaw from the draft. "We need him back here; he makes this base work." When Dad walked through the front door the next night, it was the first time I saw Mother cry.

Red and his crew were jacks of all trades. They knew that with Christmas coming there would be a shortage of toys because the material required was going into the war effort, so they stayed after work and turned out toy guns, doll carriages, wagons, and scooters for the base kids.

It was an adventurous time for a four-year-old. We'd often take picnics at the base of the newly completed Mount Rushmore with its four presidents looking down on us, including Abraham Lincoln. Grandma Ethel would always say, "I'm taking extra Kleenex in case Abe has a cold."

Red's reputation as Mr. Fixit had gotten around. A rural couple near the base hired him to convert an aged Ford truck into a homemade tractor. He spent Saturdays installing bigger tires, replacing the engine with one more powerful, welding on a forklift. I joined him not to help with the mechanics but to be free for lunch, which in the rural tradition was a big meal of fried chicken, mashed potatoes, and Jell-O with whipped cream, just as it had been during Dad's working days with Oscar on another farm.

In Igloo everyone kept track of the daily war news. Mother said years later that she had a hair appointment when news of the D Day invasion of France broke on the radio. She never forgot that her hairdresser was sobbing when Mother arrived. The young woman's fiancé was in the 82nd Airborne, the tip of the spear in Normandy. He had jumped in behind enemy lines with the 82nd. All the dispatches from Normandy in the opening days of the invasion were highly dramatic, but they didn't begin to reflect the chaos, the savage fighting, which was often face-to-face, the maddeningly slow pace of advances by the Allied forces.

On American movie screens, in radio dispatches and newspaper accounts, the descriptions were factual, but they could not measure up to the brutal, bloody reality of the greatest military confrontation in history. Weeks later, mother's hairdresser unexpectedly received a package from her fiancé, who had survived the invasion. It was a parachute with instructions to have it made into a wedding dress.

Meanwhile I was wearing a junior Army helmet every day and waging war with toy guns from

sagebrush cover, base barricades, and sloughs (pro-
nounced "slews"), the groundwater pools in the
prairie.

Although Igloo, officially titled the Black Hills
Ordnance Depot, was initially a pop-up base with
no luxuries, the Army had managed to construct a
movie theater, a dance hall, a gym attached to the
school (which served grades one through twelve),
and a PX, a general store open to civilians as well
as uniform personnel while the war raged across the
Atlantic and the Pacific.

Everyone, military personnel and civilians alike,
felt they had a role in fighting these distant enemies.
News of the war in that distant corner of America
was dispatched on radio, Movietone News in the
movie theaters, and in the weekly editions of **Time**
and **Life** magazines.

It was an era of big dance bands, and a number
of them made their way to Igloo. At Christmas, the
base put on a big holiday show, and at age four, I
was chosen to open the evening. I was standing in a
cavernous auditorium clouded with cigarette smoke,
looking out on an audience consisting mostly of men
in military uniforms. I could see my dad at the back
of the hall holding up a silver dollar, which I would
get if he could hear me. I can remember only the
opening line: "They said I was too young to speak
a piece tonight . . ." But it must have gone well, for
when I finished and raced to Dad, he handed over

the silver dollar. It was my first experience speaking for money, and I managed to extend the gratification for a long time.

Another memory that Mother often repeated: She had pulled into the post-office parking lot and told me to stay in the car. I protested. Mother wanted to know why I was insisting on going into the post of-fice. She said I thought for a moment and then said, "I've never seen the floor in there." When I became a globe-trotting journalist, Mother would often say, "I should have seen that coming in the Igloo post office."

Mother was now managing a family of five, in-cluding my two young brothers, in a tiny house in which she gave baby baths to infant Mike in a wash-tub atop a small kitchen table.

**U.S. Army munitions bunkers,
Edgemont, South Dakota**

When Germany surrendered, the Igloo base erupted in celebration, spilling over into the neighboring town of Edgemont, a cowboy and sheep-herder favorite in the sagebrush prairie. Dad loaded us into the 1939 Ford and drove us to town. It wasn't Times Square, but the joy was the same. The small-town streets were jammed with locals and uniformed men and women from the base.

Then came the nuclear bombs dropped on Japan. The war was ended by the most powerful weapons ever created. The nuclear age had arrived, and the devastation was so catastrophic that the lingering challenge is to keep them from ever being used again. However, the proliferation of nuclear weapons around the world comes with no guarantee.

America went into high gear to meet the needs of the men and women who were coming home. Igloo was on its way to becoming a curiosity in the sagebrush. As for the Brokaw family, Dad wanted to go to Texas and the oil patch where his operational and mechanical skills would have been in high demand.

Mother wisely said, "Texas is a long way from our family. The Corps of Engineers is building a huge dam on the Missouri River. You have government credits for your wartime service. I think we should go there."

And so we did.

PART II

CHAPTER 11

Building the Fort Randall Dam

THE COUNTRY EXPLODED with new construction of housing, towns, schools, shopping centers, and highways, and factories converting from military weapons to peacetime requirements.

The Brokaws were on the move again. Mother and Dad squeezed all of our belongings into a two-wheel trailer hooked up to our 1939 Ford. The three Brokaw boys were put in the back seat, and we headed east. We crossed the southern Black Hills, drove through the Pine Ridge reservation, over a bridge crossing the Missouri River and onto the site of what would become one of the largest dams in North America.

It was called Fort Randall, the name of a long-abandoned nineteenth-century U.S. Cavalry post across the river. Its most famous resident had been Sitting Bull, the legendary Sioux leader who was imprisoned there with members of his family and others from his tribe.

Sitting Bull had been the presiding chief of the large Sioux encampment in Little Bighorn, Montana, when Lieutenant Colonel George Armstrong Custer foolishly attacked the gathered tribes. The tribes, led by the fearless leader Crazy Horse, responded with a deadly fury, wiping out Custer and his men.

It was a colossal defeat, yet a thriving community in the Black Hills is named Custer and no town is called Sitting Bull or Crazy Horse. But there is a private monumental statue of Crazy Horse erected by an American sculptor of Polish origin, Korczak Ziolkowski. The Crazy Horse Memorial is a kind of perpetual work in progress. It's been under way since 1948, and it was commissioned by local Sioux tribes angry that four white American presidents have Mount Rushmore but there were no plans for Native American leaders. The work on the Crazy Horse Memorial is all financed by private donations and the enterprise remains in the hands of the Ziolkowski family with generous help from a South Dakota entrepreneur, T. Denny Sanford.

In 1946, when we arrived at what would become our new home in south central South Dakota, Dad took me to a bluff overlooking the untamed Missouri River and said, "They're going to build one of the biggest dams in America right here." I was only seven, but skeptical. This raw, unbroken country with steep gullies and tall riverbanks formed by deep chalk bluffs was a major challenge.

It was Lewis and Clark country. More than a

Fort Randall Dam construction, 1954

hundred years earlier the famous team of explorers had paddled their way through this country headed to the Pacific coast, a monumental achievement that took their hearty fellow explorers more than two years to complete. Now, in the mid-twentieth century, the word was out about the prospects of good construction jobs at good wages, so the two adjoining counties and the Yankton Sioux reservation were in play, but local businessmen and tribal elders were skeptical. They didn't believe the three small towns close to the site could handle the flood of workers and their families who would be arriving to work on the dam.

So the U.S. Army Corps of Engineers took a bold step. It decided to build from scratch a postmodern town to handle the expected three thousand newcomers. Families from Mississippi, Oklahoma, North Carolina, Illinois, Minnesota, Iowa, and Nebraska, as well as North and South Dakota, were expected.

There was nothing quite like it on the Great Plains. Fort Randall was more than a construction project; it was a monument to working-class America. Ninety percent of the population was blue collar, survivors of the Great Depression and then of World War II. When **Life** magazine did a photo spread on the town and the dam, we knew we were in the promised land.

The government named the new town on the river Pickstown after Lewis Pick, the Corps of Engineers general in charge, and immediately began construction of a postmodern town of graceful boulevards, two- and three-bedroom duplexes with garages, a trailer park that could handle two hundred mobile homes, and an arc at the edge of town for permanent homes for the white-collar families of engineers.

They also built a new school with state-of-the-art laboratories and equipment for gymnastics that we didn't know how to use. A stately church with a steeple anchored one corner of the town square. The altar was on a rotation that revealed a Catholic, Jewish, and Protestant setting as needed. The community centerpiece was a town traffic circle with an American flag anchored in the grassy island. On one side was a commercial district containing a large drugstore with a popular fountain, and a bakery, barbershop, and the post office. The other half had a dry goods store, a large grocery store, meeting rooms for local civic groups, and a full-service garage.

The Corps of Engineers wisely decided the town would have no bars or liquor stores. The community mission was to work night and day to build the dam, not to drink.

The movie theater was the largest for fifty miles. An eight-lane bowling alley, spacious pool table room, and snack bar were just next door. A model hospital and dentistry office were fully staffed. All of that on a rolling-hills section of the prairie where two years earlier there had been widely scattered cabins owned by Sioux tribal members, a couple of ranches, rattlesnakes, coyotes, and jackrabbits. It's hard to believe, but the cost of construction for the entire town of Pickstown was just over nine million dollars, now the price of some individual homes in Malibu, California. There was no town quite like it on the Great Plains.

We were like a founding family. With work on the dam going nonstop, the payroll was flush, and the population was hungry for goods, from furniture to wardrobes to cars, after the lean war years and the Depression before that.

Grandma and Grandpa moved into the large trailer park, occupying a small one-bedroom trailer. I'd often join them as they listened to major league baseball games on the radio. When the national

Mother and Grandpa Jim

anthem was played, Grandpa's Irish genes would kick in and he'd begin to choke up. Grandma Ethel would always say, "For God's sake, Jim, stop it!"

Jim had a job on the dam site, directing dump trucks where to unload. He remained a shy, emotional Irishman despite Ethel's scolding. When he attended school programs where I was performing a comic reading, I could hear his guffaws, which would give way to muffled sobs of pride, followed by Grandma's instructions to be quiet. Grandpa Jim died before his time, a man broken by the penalties of the Great Depression.

Grandma Ethel lived into her eighties, always a lively presence in our family. When Elvis Presley burst onto the scene Mother and Dad were appalled, while my brothers and I were immediate fans. Grandma watched Presley on television and declared, "He seems like a nice young man. I hope he makes a lot of money." Elvis must have heard her.

Later, Grandma visited a Minneapolis school friend she had not seen in half a century. The friend had an elegant beachfront home in La Jolla, California. As they embraced, I thought of all Grandma had been through without a complaint. The Depression on the farm. The Army base. Living in a trailer house with little money. But here she was with her wealthy friend, laughing and recalling their Minneapolis childhood as if it were yesterday.

In 1950, Dad bought his first new car after a long line of used cars dating back to Ford's Model T. The new car was a standard Chevrolet sedan, battleship gray, no radio, with four doors and a GM small engine. He still had little use for bells and whistles.

America went through a sharp recession in 1949, but it had little effect on the Fort Randall Dam construction or the twenty-four-seven shifts of workers. Western Construction Company took big projects to a new level by buying a fleet of massive dump trucks, the largest in the world, and an equally impressive

**The largest dump trucks in the world,
called Ukes, short for Euclid, excavating
the Missouri River fill in the early stages
of the Fort Randall Dam**

array of gigantic electronic shovels to fill them. The
shovels scooped up truckloads of dirt with one bite
and offloaded it into the waiting trucks, which had
enough capacity to level a river bluff within a week.
The trucks were called Ukes, short for Euclid. It took
two rail flatcars to transport just one truck, which
had a sticker price of $70,000.

Western bought twenty of the first models, which
were powered by two 300-horsepower engines

**Mammoth shovels that could
fill a Uke in four bites**

running simultaneously. They were so mechanically efficient it took new drivers just a few days to master the hydraulic steering wheel, and the clutch was automatic. At the end of a ten-hour shift, seventy-six grease fittings were checked and every four weeks there was another inspection to tighten bolts loosened by the rocky rides. One tire cost $1,400. The equally impressive electric shovels, which cost $150,000 apiece, could fill a truck with just four bites.

To see the monsters in the hands of skilled operators was like watching a dinosaur-and-elephant ballet.

The best operators and truck drivers came from all over the country. Two very large brothers, who traced their heritage to Finland, came down from northern Minnesota quarries every summer to pilot the trucks.

Pickstown quickly became a popular tourist attraction for the surrounding population, made up of people who lived in small, aged communities with minuscule budgets. In contrast, all of our streets were paved and maintained by a full-time professional crew—including Red, who invented a sand spreader for icy roads. The town fathers were so impressed with it that they sent over an engineer to get the blueprints. There were none. Dad could only explain his invention by taking the visitor out to his garage and walking him through the idea and parts.

The famed explorers Lewis and Clark had town streets named for them, but there was no tribute for the Sioux Indian nation, even though Pickstown sat in the middle of the tribe's territory. Later, when the town wanted to name a street for me, I suggested instead that a prominent Lakota Sioux should have the honor. I was quickly turned down.

The work on the dam went on morning, noon, and night for ten years. Taming the Missouri and altering its function was a monumental task that would bring not only flood control to that stretch of the river and its long reach upstream, but would also create one of the largest lakes in the Midwest, with its boating and fishing opportunities, and supply electrical power for hundreds of miles across the Midwest.

Everyone in Pickstown knew all the worker shifts—daytime, swing (4:00 P.M. to midnight), graveyard (midnight to 8:00 A.M.), and families arranged their activities so as not to disturb the neighbors' sleep patterns. There were skilled heavy-equipment operators on those massive shovels, Caterpillars, and other earth-moving equipment, who worked with welders, electricians, riveters, carpenters, surveyors, and engineers. Wages and overtime were also part of the daily scuttlebutt. This was a generation raised on Great Depression uncertainty, and so the shift to a steady paycheck was a relief and the object of a lot of comment. Workers were inclined to let their friends know how much they earned in overtime the preceding week.

**Fort Randall chapel, Pickstown,
South Dakota**

Families moved in and out, depending on the phases of construction. We made friends in a hurry, and over the years Pickstown School has staged memorable reunions for long-separated classmates. The roster of success is long and varied. Most students were from working-class families, and a common goal was to be the first in your family to attend college. My generation of students is laced with GE executives, orthopedists, orthodontists, authors, coaches, airline pilots, industrial managers, engineers, and teachers. Others went into the construction business or the military, where they were selected for skilled assignments such as air traffic control. It was before young women had an equal shot at education recognition, but the smartest students in most grades were girls. In the junior high spelling bee, I was matched for the title against Susie Wardell, and I knew I was doomed. I was not wrong.

At our school reunions, it was an uplifting experience to see the personal and professional success of so many Pickstown graduates. It was a snapshot of the economic and social evolution of opportunity in parts of postwar America. Even those who had spent only a year in Pickstown returned to say it was the best experience of their families' lives. It was what our parents dreamed of during the dark days of the Depression and World War II, and it came true. It was going on across America. The federal workforce doubled in the fifties. State and local government workforces tripled.

**Pickstown, South Dakota, 1949,
construction finished**

Homes in Pickstown, South Dakota

In a way, Pickstown was a model for the can-do spirit of America. It was, alas, a time when racial discrimination was still a hard fact of life. The Pickstown population was mostly Caucasian, and included a few families from the Deep South, but the subject of race rarely came up in white-bread South Dakota back then, in large part because the Great Plains Black population was, at most, minuscule.

Mother and Dad raised us to be colorblind. Dad was not a big sports fan, but to my brothers and me he often cited his heroes as Jackie Robinson, Joe Louis, and Jesse Owens. He didn't follow sports news except when the great Joe Louis was defending his heavyweight title. Later, I realized his experience with discrimination as a school dropout with learning challenges broadened his attitude toward other people.

Jackie Robinson became my favorite athlete and role model. I didn't meet him until he retired and was campaigning for New York's Nelson Rockefeller, a presidential candidate who was an early promoter of ending racial discrimination. When Robinson accompanied Rockefeller into the studio where I would be doing an interview, I was so thrilled and surprised I all but knocked over Rockefeller to shake hands with my hero. Over the years, I stayed in touch with his widow, Rachel Robinson, who ran a scholarship program in his name. She had been at his side during the difficult years and was an elegant, indispensable ally.

In Pickstown, as in most of America, we were still

stuck in the antiquated ways of dealing with race. **Amos 'n' Andy** was a popular radio show, with white performers playing Black friends to a large radio audience as they had been since the thirties. A Fort Randall town official and his family were enthusiasts of the great American musical, so they staged an elaborate production of **Show Boat.** Many in the cast were in blackface and no one raised any objection. Years later, at our reunions, we'd ask each other, "Good God, how embarrassing was that?"

A number of the families were Southerners, and one day a mother from Mississippi was freely using the N-word to describe Black people as she drove her son, me, and other friends to a baseball game. From the back seat, I objected loudly. We got into a heated argument, and she said, "Well, you northerners call creeks 'cricks'"—which is true—and I laughed, saying "So?" I was maybe twelve at the time but I wouldn't give up. Finally, she drove me home, opened the door, and said, "Get out."

In Pickstown in the fifties, the local baseball team was made up of military veterans and quickly became the best amateur team in eastern South Dakota. Players from Texas, Oklahoma, and the Midwest whose careers had been cut short by the war were still fit and competitive. They wiped up the local competition and faltered only when they took on a semi-pro team of college stars heading to the majors.

Television signals had not yet reached our corner of South Dakota, but there was no absence of entertainment. America had traveling troupes of performers. The All American Red Heads were an all-women's basketball team who were gifted, and Pickstown's men were former high school and college players who had not lost their touch during the war years.

Touring wrestlers and boxers brought something new: two African American boxers who chose to stay in the high school locker room rather than mingle. I became their errand boy, retrieving sandwiches and soft drinks from the local drugstore. The boxers were New York pros, one of whom had been promising until he was caught in a fixed fight. Now he was relegated to touring small towns in the Midwest.

That day, they seemed relieved to have an eager volunteer, and they insisted on tipping me. After their staged exhibition on a small-town baseball diamond at night, they left, relieved, I am sure, to get the hell out of that town in the middle of nowhere. When they were gone, I'd scour the boxing publications, hoping to see that the penalized boxer had been excused for his early mistake. One day his name popped up as a restored competitor. I was thrilled.

The most bizarre visitors were the donkey baseball teams. A truckload of donkeys and their handlers arrived to take on the locals. The batter would get a hit, mount a donkey, and then ride it around the bases. So far, no corner of the National Baseball Hall of Fame has been set aside for donkey baseball.

When work was at full throttle on the dam, the workers had newfound prosperity, and that touched off the most generous Christmas most families had ever experienced. New wardrobes and bikes or, yes, shotguns for the young hunting crowd. Mother and Dad must have been hoping for a doctor, because I received a chemistry set and a microscope. Neither escaped a dark corner of the attic.

Mother and Dad were frugal and conservative in their family plans, but in 1951 they surprised my brothers and me. Dad had a plan. We would be going to California in the new car to visit Dad's brother, Richard, and his family.

Until then, the big family trip had been to Minneapolis. This time we'd stay with friends from the construction days as we made our way across Wyoming and on to Utah, Nevada, and California.

This was before seatbelts, so Dad built a platform in the back seat for the three boys, their comic books, sports magazines, and occasional wrestling matches—until Red would sweep his muscular forearm over the seat as Mother would urge us to look at the glories of Yellowstone National Park or the Teton mountain range.

Salt Lake City, the home of the Mormon Church, the eighteenth-century pilgrimage to this promised land, was for our family of mainstream Christian protestants at once mystical, admirable, and enterprising. Polite guides, dressed as if for temple, were quietly eager to answer questions about the origin of the faith, the rituals, and the expectations for members.

It was the beginning of a personal admiration for the church and its expectations of members. Much later, I was honored to be asked to host the Church's annual Christmas service in Salt Lake City.

En route to California, as a construction family living on a large dam site on the Missouri River, we felt compelled to visit the majestic Hoover Dam holding back the Colorado River, on the border of Arizona and Nevada. It was named for President Herbert Hoover. When his presidency cratered, leading to the Great Depression, there was a movement to change the dam's name to Boulder. It remains Hoover.

We scooted by Las Vegas and headed for Long Beach and Uncle Richard and family. Red and Richard were in a much better place than they had been when the only choice was whatever bed was empty in the cold Brokaw House Hotel in Bristol.

Rich, after his service in the Coast Guard and the Navy during the war, got a job at the Long Beach post office and became one of the most successful Boy Scouts leaders in the United States. His troops of working-class scouts were well known for their record number of promotions to Eagle Scout, the highest honor in scouting.

Our trip to California was a seminal experience. We were all thrilled by the mix of sea, flora, and fauna and the wide range of topography. Coastal beaches gave way to fertile soil for a variety of fruit trees and other groves, stretching to the sharp rise of mountain ranges that gave way to vast deserts. Disneyland was still in the planning stage, but we had a big day at Knott's Berry Farm, a working farm and sprawling tourist attraction in Orange County founded in the thirties. It's still going, with a ghost town, carnival ride, cafés, and a large market of California goods. It is also the show-business birthplace of Steve Martin, who performed his banjo act there at the beginning of his career.

I joined Mother and Dad on a tour that included a popular television quiz show called **Queen for a Day.** We made a trip to Farmers Market in Hollywood, an outdoor pavilion chock-full of fresh papayas, avocados, oranges, baked goods, and woven baskets. It made an instant impression on me. When I moved to California as a grown-up, I went right back to the market. I was relieved to see it had lost none of its allure.

We made a side trip to Tijuana, Mexico, and to the celebrated San Diego Zoo. At the time, California was just beginning its explosive growth, so it was still manageable for those of us from the prairie, and it was not hard to see the appeal.

From Los Angeles, Dad steered north to San Francisco, where Mother was eager to ride a cable car, believing they would match the funiculars in Swiss ski resorts.

She was puzzled when she didn't see any, so she

asked a conductor on what appeared to be a conventional trolley, "Where are the cable cars?"

"Lady," he said, "this is as close as you're going to get. This **is** a cable car."

We had another memorable experience when Mother took me to a J. C. Penney store for a new pair of shoes. We were approached by a dapper short man who asked, "Do you know who I am?"

Mother said, "Yes. You're J. C. Penney. I just read your biography in the **Minneapolis Tribune.** We're here to buy my son a new pair of shoes."

He seemed pleased and immediately summoned a clerk.

"Boy," I thought, "I'm going to get a free new pair of shoes."

Instead, he instructed the clerk to sell us a pair of shoes. J.C. didn't get to be a very successful merchant by giving away the goods.

We were bedazzled by San Francisco's hilly charm, its elegant shopping squares, all framed by the bay and the Golden Gate Bridge, never imagining that one day all three of Meredith's and my daughters would live and work there at one time or another.

When we returned to Pickstown, all that seemed impossible to realize in our working-class culture. By then, Native American families who lived on the Yankton Sioux reservation along the Missouri River were being squeezed out by the construction of the Fort Randall Dam, which would flood their properties on the river bottom. They were compensated for their losses, but at a minimal rate. The tribe fought a long, unsuccessful battle for much greater remuneration. One of the families—the Highrock clan—lived on a fertile piece of Missouri River bottomland, where they kept a garden to complement the fish they caught and the rewards of their traplines.

Sylvan Highrock was a handsome, athletic Sioux who became a close friend. He stayed with us in town from time to time when the weather was severe. My mother always said he was the most polite of all my schoolboy friends. His mother dressed in shawls and moccasins when she came to town to watch Sylvan play basketball. One winter she sewed bunny tails into my store-bought cap because she thought it wasn't warm enough.

When I invited Sylvan to join Dad and me at a regional baseball playoff, he was plainly shy in the all-white crowd. I'll always remember he had two one-dollar bills tucked into a matchbox as a billfold.

When our junior high basketball team went to a Sioux boarding school to play all-Indian teams, Sylvan was our only Sioux teammate. He would always counsel, "Don't let these guys bother you. We're just as good." Wrong. Those players were on their home court year round, and they knew every angle. We never won.

When the dam advanced, it raised the Missouri River water level and flooded out the Sioux properties, so the Highrocks moved west to another reservation near Winner, South Dakota. Unbeknownst to me, before they moved, Sylvan got a summer job in the cavernous intake tunnels of the Fort Randall Dam. He had no hearing protection, and the tunnels were massive echo chambers. By the end of summer, he was stone deaf.

When I found him a few years later in Winner, he had dropped out of school, was drinking heavily, and was working on a garbage truck.

But his first words to me were, "Do you remember when I hit two home runs in a game and got free movie tickets?"

His father, who was standing nearby, became nervous when Sylvan began disparaging the local white community. He said, "Sylvan doesn't mean that," knowing there could be reprisals.

In South Dakota the two worlds, American Indian and Caucasian, remain separate and unequal, divided by race, culture, and history. Sylvan and I had an awkward reunion and farewell, so far removed from our carefree adolescence.

Before I left, I asked if his family spoke their native language at home when we were kids. He nodded.

"How come I didn't know that?" I asked.

He gave me a small smile and said, "We had to keep something from you white boys."

Not long after, I heard that Sylvan was gone. He was not yet forty.

During a trip back to South Dakota as an adult, I drove across the Pine Ridge Sioux reservation and stopped at the home of an Indian who was selling local art. Roger Scabby Face was sitting beneath a homespun shade made of willow branches. He had a droll sense of humor, not unusual in the Sioux culture. When I pointed to the willow branches and said, "I can't remember what you call this," Roger looked the willows over, turned to me, and said, "We Indians call it 'shade.'"

It wasn't until I left that part of South Dakota that I fully realized the conflicted role of the Sioux in relation to the nineteenth-century U.S. Army base just across the river from the dam. All that was left of the base was the skeletal remains of the chapel, which by then was a ghostly chalk structure.

The legendary Sioux chief Sitting Bull, along with his wives and families, had been held as prisoners on the base within their own tented compound. Later, Sitting Bull was transferred to a jail in North Dakota, where he was killed by Union soldiers in a clash that grew out of a rebellion by a young Sioux. He was believed to be in his mid- or late fifties.

In Pickstown, we were surprised when a Native American family moved into a home reserved for the workers. The Welch family had two sons who were exceptional in every way. They were dressed in preppy clothes, including loafers and khakis. The rest of us were in sneakers and blue jeans. The son my age—Jimmy—became a close friend, and we were on the same baseball team. When I said something about "you Sioux" he quickly corrected me. "Tom, my family is Blackfoot, from Montana."

Jim and his brother were good students and good athletes. Jim's father had a high-tech, high-paying welding job on the dam and qualified for the upgraded housing. When his work was finished, the Welch family moved on and we lost track, until one Sunday morning when I was living in Washington, D.C., in my early thirties. **The New York Times Book Review** had a front-page rave review for a new book by a Montana Native American: James Welch.

Meredith at first thought it was a coincidence, but I was sure it was my old friend. I called the publisher, and Jim and I had a joyful reunion on the **Today** show when I said, "What are the chances two members of Mr. Holmes's seventh-grade class in South Dakota would become bestselling authors?" We stayed in touch while his reputation as a novelist, essayist, and poet soared. When he died too early, of heart disease and lung cancer, I went to the funeral with my friend Tom McGuane, the celebrated Montana author, who was also a friend and admirer of Jim's.

During the Pickstown years, America was undergoing a historic modernization. Later, some of my working-class friends told me Pickstown was the first home in which they had indoor plumbing. One of my hearty pals lived in a small trailer home with his parents, and his "bedroom" was an unheated addition to the exterior. That's where he slept through the coldest winter nights. The newest models of trailer homes had an elevated roof that served as an extra, cramped bedroom for the kids.

On weekends, we became accustomed to our streets filling up with local tourists driving slowly through this modern wonderland as we stayed cool, privileged occupants of a miracle on the prairie.

One of our seasonal visitors to Pickstown was Dad's early patron, Oscar Johnson. His friends would drop him off, and Oscar would have the same wardrobe: a new flannel shirt and overalls. He'd sleep on the living room couch and leaf through back copies of **The Saturday Evening Post** and **Life** while Mother would say, laughing, "What do we do with him today?"

Oscar was so deaf he heard none of her inquiry. When there was a big snow, Oscar was a happy man. He would grab a shovel and clear the sidewalks and driveway with strong rhythmic strokes, pausing only to clap his hands to activate circulation in limbs that had been frozen so often. Then he'd look down and give me a toothy smile.

When Oscar died, he left a tidy estate of land, machinery, and older cars amounting to about $200,000. Dad was the executor and beneficiary if there were no living relatives. Turns out Oscar had two sisters in their nineties who got it all. As I told Dad, we were not meant to have easy money.

Our other regular visitors were Dad's bachelor brother, John, and unmarried sisters Celia and Ann. They shared a house and a Buick sedan in Bristol.

John ran the municipal liquor store, while Celia and Ann worked in a creamery, which meant they always had a faint odor of sour milk when their workday was over. They all had the Brokaw family hearing loss, so conversation was high-decibel. After a weekend, they'd return to Bristol, but not before giving each of Red's sons a silver dollar. One year I gave them a fossil I had found on the Missouri River shores. I think it became a family heirloom.

I adored them for many reasons, not the least of which was their pride in their baby brother, Red, who began life with everyone writing him off. He was the emblematic, prized blue-collar success in this modern miracle on the prairie.

Construction projects with populations similar to that of Fort Randall were underway across America. While the G.I. Bill, the federal government's education provision that helped vets who wanted to become doctors, lawyers, teachers, and engineers, was filling white-collar needs, the Fort Randall Dam and other construction projects were doing the same for the blue-collar set.

Mother worked in the Pickstown post office, which in a way fulfilled her early dream of becoming a journalist. In a community where everyone had arrived from elsewhere, she was a friendly audience for tales "from back home," which she then shared with me during dinner. She noticed the mother of a friend I admired had a wad of cash in her purse. When Mother commented on it, my friend's mother said, "I never know when he may leave me," referring to my friend's father. It was a jarring reality for me, the child of stable parents in a community of transient workers.

Red was the go-to man in the town's maintenance department, plowing snow in the winter, paving streets and building parks in the summer. Weekends he was often hired by dam contractors for his Caterpillar skills. His Corps of Engineers job qualified him for a new three-bedroom duplex with a modern kitchen, utility room, and garage. The rooms were small by modern standards, but for families shaped by the Depression and the construction constraints imposed by the demands of World War II, they were majestic. Moreover, the town landlord was the U.S. Army Corps of Engineers, so if the heat went off or the electricity, we'd just dial the town maintenance shop and skilled workers would arrive shortly.

Mother and Dad's friends from their days on other construction sites became regular visitors to this magic place on the prairie where the dam was a twenty-four-seven attraction. We'd squeeze two families of five into three small bedrooms, with the kids camped on the living room floor and couch. Weekends were spent sightseeing and picnicking along the Missouri River overlooking the constant construction of the dam.

Our first neighbors in a shared duplex were country music fans from southern Illinois, and they played a steady concert of Johnny Cash and the other big country stars of the fifties. At first, Mother, much more the Glenn Miller and Artie Shaw type, was not happy. But before long she couldn't wait to hear more Cash or Eddy Arnold and Gene Autry. Whenever I hear those artists now, I think of the Dalton family.

Red, who had such a difficult start in life, was in his element. He had a fleet of the latest big maintenance machinery at his disposal. He especially liked firing up a big snowplow and liberating ranchers in the middle of a blizzard. One night he came home with one eye still frozen shut from the open cockpit on the snow blade. He laughed it off.

In warmer weather, our yard was his canvas, with a homemade picnic table, two Red-made lawn chairs, and a trellis for a climbing vine. Part of the family lore: He went out onto the riverbanks and found a young Chinese elm tree, which he dug up and brought home to our backyard. It didn't quite fit into the hole he had dug so he whipped out his knife, cut off several roots, and stomped on others to make them fit.

Mother famously said, "If that tree lives, I'll eat my hat."

After Mother and Dad were gone, I drove by our old lot some sixty years later and the elm was still there, aged and stooped but standing. Dad's revenge.

Mother learned not to say aloud she needed a household appliance—a new ironing board, say—because Red would rush to his workshop and build her one. She wanted **something** from a store or Sears catalog.

His most famous creation was a homemade power lawn mower for my thriving mowing business. He found wheels off an old wagon, a sturdy plywood platform, and a small motor from a washing machine, and he welded handles from leftover pipe. He fashioned blades from some discarded steel sections and I was in business. The mower went through everything; it was well fitted for a community in which families were constantly moving in and out, leaving behind overgrown lawns and runaway weeds. Finally, after five years of tough jobs, the faithful mower blew a rod, and by then I had moved on to summer camp jobs as a lifeguard.

A long stretch of fertile prairie behind the neighborhood garage became a community garden and, of course, Mother and Dad had a productive patch of strawberries, tomatoes, potatoes, corn, and rhubarb. Autumn was canning season. Mother was celebrated for her dill pickles. Dad would freeze a few quarts of strawberries, and in the middle of the long winters we'd thaw them just enough to leave a thin sheet of ice for a kind of prairie glacé.

At some point we shared a driveway with the Everest family, a Midwestern clan that was quietly making a name with big construction projects. Mr. Everest was out the door and on the job at 6:45 every morning. For the Everests, little known outside the Midwest, this was the family's biggest contract ever. They had coal and quarry holdings in Illinois and South Dakota and were quietly becoming a major construction force.

They were all business and not much involved in the local working class, the Corps of Engineers, or commercial enterprises. They enlisted Mother to help with entertaining from time to time, and I'll always remember her coming home with a new leftover dish: crêpes suzette, alcohol-infused thin pancakes. I was about twelve at the time and Mother treated this as a coming-of-age experience. We shared the suzettes before supper. I am confident no other working-class family in town was sampling crêpes suzette that evening, much less a mother and son.

After five years in Pickstown, Dad began to have brutal, piercing back pain as a result of lifting anything and everything: machinery, wooden rowboats he was impatient to launch, tractor tires, even the back ends of small cars he wanted repositioned. I have this fixed image of a scorching hot summer dusk, at the end of a workday, Red sitting at our small dining table, an iced tea in hand, in his undershirt, staring blankly at a distant wall. The undershirt had an angular bulge. It was a rib broken long ago and never fixed. We called it his hat rack.

But now he had a more serious problem: His lower back was a mess after all those years of heavy lifting. He was in terrible pain and needed surgery. Back surgery was entering a new era and he volunteered. It required a bone transplant in the spinal area, and once completed, the surgery meant two months of round-the-clock bed rest. So in the middle of a hot, no-air-conditioning South Dakota summer, Dad spent long days flat on his back or on his stomach. While Mother continued her post office work, every eight hours my brothers Bill and Mike and I would roll him over so he was either faceup or facedown for the next phase.

**The majestic Fort Randall Dam
on the Missouri River, 1950s**

Later, when back surgery had vastly improved, he had a second surgery at the Mayo Clinic in Minnesota. He emerged pain-free and this time played by the rules and never again had difficulty.

But in that earlier summer, in addition to the physical ordeal, Dad worried constantly about his working future. The Fort Randall Dam was close to completion, so Pickstown would be shutting down almost all of its residential neighborhoods and selling off the remnants.

What Dad didn't know was that the project's chief engineer—the civilian equivalent of a commanding general—was a big fan of Mother and Dad, their work skills and homespun values. George and Laura Evans were gracious Southerners who presided over this monumental project with its mix of white-collar engineers and blue-collar masters of complex electrical grids, X-ray welding, the largest trucks, and massive shovels with buckets large enough to lift an automobile. On Sundays the white-collar executives and engineers worshipped side by side with the blue-collar workers. The New Year's Eve celebration brought the whole town together for a dance in the spotless main garage with snowplows and tractors moved aside.

Even so, we all knew there was a dividing line— white-collar college graduates and the rest of us. So it was a surprise when George Evans showed up at our duplex just as Dad was beginning to recover from that bedridden summer. Mr. Evans told Mother and Dad

Fort Randall Dam

that their next posting would be on a dam downriver, Gavins Point Dam in Yankton, South Dakota. Red would be promoted to foreman and be responsible for developing the campgrounds and recreational facilities, maintaining the roads around the dam, and clearing winter snow.

My god, for the tough little kid from Bristol this was a bonanza. Mother was equally happy because Yankton had excellent public and Catholic schools, two colleges, a good hospital, and a vibrant commercial district. It also had one of the most powerful radio stations in the Midwest, WNAX, where Lawrence Welk got his start as the house band director.

Many years later, I met Welk in California and told him of our common connection to Yankton. He got excited and wanted to give me something. It was a tiny wooden bowling pin from his Palm Springs bowling alley. His reputation for tightfisted money management was secure.

PART III

Main Street, Yankton

Bridge over the Missouri River

CHAPTER 12

Yankton and Meredith

YANKTON WAS CALLED THE MOTHER CITY of the Dakotas because it was the first town on the river leading into the Great Plains.

Lewis and Clark had passed through the area when it was the home territory of a peaceful band of the Lakota Sioux tribe. That tribe warned that another band three hundred miles upriver was not so friendly, it was large and well armed with spears and bows and arrows. Nonetheless, the Lewis and Clark expedition made it through the Oglala territory with some tense confrontations but no warfare.

The arrival of Lewis and Clark signaled a new era. The white men were coming.

Later, Lieutenant Colonel George Custer had a summer encampment in Yankton. A welcoming billboard in town advertised the Custer connection. A large representation of Custer was on the billboard, with the caption, "Shore wish I had stayed."

Gavins Point Dam spillway

Missouri River looking downstream

Yankton became the Brokaw family home of record. Mother and Dad had been careful stewards of their money, and they were able to buy a two-story home on a corner lot for $11,500. They were prepared to pay cash as a result of their management of two incomes—Dad's work on the dam, town streets, and parks and Mother's job in the post office. They wisely decided to accept favorable loan terms from the bank and invest the leftovers in bonds and mutual funds, a new experience for these children of hard times.

At Gavins Point Dam, Red had a crew of can-do masons, carpenters, electricians, and machinery operators. They were short on blueprints but long on experience as they made the area into one of the most popular weekend destinations in South Dakota and Nebraska. The campgrounds were impeccably maintained and organized. Later, friends from as far away as Omaha said Gavins Point was their favorite family retreat. I was not surprised. After I left Yankton, whenever I returned for a visit Dad would get me to join him for a nocturnal inspection of the parks to make sure all was in order.

On Saturdays he continued to work at our home in town, 1515 Mulberry Street, with its all-American address that matched the homespun character of the neighborhood. The house needed some touching up, which for Red was like an invitation to a do-it-yourself ball. A family friend, a Harvard student, watched in amazement as Red enlarged the garage by eyeballing the frame and then attacking it with hand tools.

In the house, he installed a second barebones bedroom and bath in the basement for my cousin Dick, who arrived from California looking for a fresh start. Dick was Uncle Rich's son, and Dad wanted to help his brother and former roommate Rich's family. Dad found Dick a job with a new company in town, a neon-sign business capitalizing on the growing market for modern advertising technology. Dick turned that opportunity into a lifetime career in the modern sign business, taking his skills back to California, where he became a supervisor for a large regional sign company.

In another corner of the basement, Dad constructed a workbench for his growing interest in furniture restoration and creating original infant rockers. The garage was also equipped with enough auto and plumbing material to handle the family needs without our having to go to a commercial enterprise. Dad never stopped working. When I had my first car, he'd ask to borrow it for an errand. That was his ruse for a test-drive to see what needed attention. One weekend he came home and said, "Your tires need alignment," which he proceeded to do with my brother Mike. He believed in doing lube jobs and oil changes in our garage instead of paying a gas station to do the job.

Mother was part of the same school. She taught her sons to do laundry and ironing, remarking it would come in handy when she was busy running a woman's shoe store on Main Street or taking an active role with the Democratic Party at election time. She was also a wise counselor to her sons as we became of dating age and a surrogate mother to pals who lost parents to cancer or heart conditions. One of them, a rascal and football star, later looked her up to tell her it was not by coincidence he showed up at our house at suppertime. She laughed and said, "Oh, Roger, I knew that. You were always welcome."

She was also a conciliator when we three boys would not measure up to Dad's standards for home chores and personal behavior. Mother would remind us of Dad's difficult upbringing and his impatience with slackers. She'd say, "You have to remember your father didn't have a childhood. He went to work instead."

Yankton was our first exposure to household television. Like most Midwestern families, we scheduled supper at 5:30 so we could dine and watch the news simultaneously. I was riveted by the opportunity to see the changing world piped into our home—especially in 1956 when NBC changed television news by twinning Chet Huntley and David Brinkley for a historic transformation from stoic single anchors to a perfectly cast combination with one in Washington and the other in New York. I watched every night, never dreaming that within ten years I would be part of the NBC team. Mother often joined me with her astute observations on politics. She retained her

Democratic Party heritage in local and national elections, even sticking with Adlai Stevenson against war hero Dwight Eisenhower.

For me, Yankton was a teenager's equivalent of winning the lottery. At the award-winning high school, I was active in sports and student-body politics. In my junior year, I shared the school-play lead with a bright, beautiful classmate whom I was destined to see a lot of in the coming years.

That same junior year, I had a classic Red moment, when I had a dispute with our coach at the state basketball tournament. The uptight coach benched me for a minor infraction in the second game, and I was distraught until I looked into the stands and saw my parents, who had battled a blizzard for two hundred miles to attend. Mother was all sympathy and concern. Red had a small smile as he draped his hand over a knee and exposed a middle finger. Bingo. Life goes on, Tom.

Later that year I was elected governor at South Dakota's Boys State, an American Legion program to expose selected high school juniors to the rewards and challenges of public service. At the same time my high school friend Meredith Auld was South Dakota's selection to attend American Legion Auxiliary's Girls Nation, where she was in a meeting with President Dwight Eisenhower.

My election came with a different bonus. I was invited to join South Dakota's famous governor on a network quiz show in New York. The governor was

Joe Foss, a World War II fighter pilot with the U.S. Marines and recipient of the Medal of Honor. He shot down a record number of Japanese war planes and sank enemy ships in the heaviest combat in the Pacific. We had clicked when he came to Boys State and heard my inaugural address. Our television appearance was in 1957, so his World War II fame was still current. With his rugged good looks and Stetson, he was a commanding figure. The show was **Two for the Money,** and the questions were fundamental subjects about American politics. We did well, winning more than six hundred dollars apiece.

When our appearance was over Governor Foss suggested I stay a few extra days to see more of New York, saying he would arrange an extension on the hotel. I called home to share the excitement of the evening and share Joe's recommendation. There was a long pause and finally Dad said, "Well, I guess so. You'll probably never get another chance to see New York City." After four days of late nights in the Village, a memorable visit to Ebbets Field where I saw my beloved Dodgers defeat the Giants, shopping at Saks, visiting the American Museum of Natural History and the Statue of Liberty, I headed home, thinking Dad was right: I'll probably never get a chance to see New York again.

Yankton was a community that celebrated the young but mostly the boys. During my three years there, two of my male friends were scholarship students at Harvard. We had two cadets at the Air Force

Academy and one at West Point. Others were re-cruited for Big Ten football teams, or they were law and medical students. They were all boys. Yet we all knew the girls were as smart or brighter. The sardonic line of the time was "Boys get a university degree. Girls get a Mrs. degree."

I was a classic case of an entitled boy who abused the privilege. After a high school record as student leader, I went off the rails and onto the party circuit, all but flunking out of the University of Iowa and doing the same when I transferred to the University of South Dakota. I took a couple of radio station jobs, but I was seriously adrift.

My high school friend Meredith Auld wrote me a blistering letter, effectively saying our friendship was over. She was especially angry after my mother stopped her one day and asked, "What do you think is going on with Tom?" Meredith and I had been leaders in our high school, and she often teased me about my "girlfriends in every port."

Another friend, who later became one of America's leading experts on the Soviet Union, agreed, saying, "We don't know what's happened to you." It was an embarrassing self-realization that I was betraying my parents and friends' confidence and expectations.

Mother came to the rescue, as usual. She was watching a Sioux City, Iowa, television station with a perfectly dreadful announcer doing the local news. She said, "You're better than he is. Go get his job." And so I did, riding a bus to Sioux City where I was paid seventy-five dollars for a six-day week as a staff announcer, weekend weather man, and occasional newscaster.

I discovered a carpool driving to the University of South Dakota Monday through Friday mornings and joined them while working and taking on a full academic load. My days started with the 6:00 A.M. commute, followed by classes until noon; then it was back to the station until 11:00 P.M. Dad was quietly relieved and helped me finance a ten-year-old well-maintained car that he knew to be reliable.

My high school friend Meredith noticed and suggested a coffee-break reunion. When she began to apologize for her earlier scolding I said, "No, I had it coming." Turns out she had recently broken up with a boyfriend, and when I casually mentioned the chance of a weekend date she agreed. One thing led to another, and we began to see each other again.

It went well. By 1962, to the surprise of most friends, we were engaged. When her sister asked, "Why Tom?" Meredith said, "I don't know if we'll have any money, but life will be interesting."

Her physician father and his partners gave a round of parties, which included regular denunciations of a national drive for government-financed medical care that Democrats were promoting. The American Medical Association unleashed a campaign led by a telegenic physician opposing the plan.

At prenuptial dinners I was the outspoken advocate of government support for medical care, in part because my beloved grandmother, Ethel, was in a locally financed facility for the elderly, with nothing more than meager Social Security checks and Mother and Dad's support. Mother, who agreed with me on the need for additional federal programs, nonetheless was concerned the wedding would be called off.

I worried Dad would tire of rushing home from work to shed his work clothes and put on a suit and tie for the round of summertime celebrations. When I raised it with him, he grinned and said, "Whose Scotch are we drinking tonight?"

When President Lyndon Johnson, in 1965, introduced his generous Medicare plan that included government-financed care for a wide range of services, it was instantly popular with the working class. The medical community quickly understood the advantages of the secure financial base. The AMA resistance disappeared overnight. Even with the government guarantees, Meredith's father, Dr. Auld, continued his quiet practice of taking care of patients who had needs beyond the government services. One Christmas I joined him as he distributed turkeys, baked goods, and presents to working-class families who needed the extra help.

The wedding took place the summer of 1962 and was a black-tie affair, attended by physicians, their families, our family, and the blue-collar friends we shared. The Aulds were serious Episcopalians, so we had a full service in the small un-air-conditioned church. When it was over—more than an hour later—I asked Grandma Ethel what she thought. She gave me a stern look and said, "If you're not married now, you never will be!"

Meredith was twenty-one. I was twenty-two. Our worldly belongings were mostly modest wedding presents, including elaborate ashtrays, that fit into the back seat of a barebones midsize Chevrolet sedan Dr. Auld had given us as a wedding present. I got a starter job as a morning anchor and editor at a conservative station in Omaha.

Meanwhile, America was modernizing from the ground up. We lived in flyover country where most highways were relics from the fifties. But President Eisenhower had initiated the Interstate Highway System, and that changed American transportation dramatically. In the American West, where we now spend so much time, the interstates are busy night and day with big commercial trucks, local delivery services, cross-country tourism, and motorcycles. State and local roadways were also upgraded and made safer.

At the same time, Mother and Dad had real security as a result of their federal government programs as they moved closer to retirement age.

At the beginning, Meredith and I were outliers in the Omaha newsroom, which reflected the city's conservative base. My newsroom colleagues were all working-class conservatives and first-rate journalists, but they couldn't believe my politics. Nebraska's two senators were Republicans, and Barry Goldwater was the presidential candidate of choice.

There was another Omaha on the north end of the city. It was the home of a substantial Black population. Black workers were key to the large meatpacking business and town maintenance in Omaha. Two of the city's most famous sons were Gale Sayers, the NFL's legendary running back, and Bob Gibson, the Hall of Fame pitcher widely regarded as one of the best ever to take the mound. I once asked Gibson if his treatment as a Black man helped fuel his fury on the mound. He answered, "You're not wrong."

What is seared in my mind is the day in Omaha when the world changed. I was finishing a morning shift as the news editor when UPI and AP news began a cacophony of alarms. Shots had been fired at President John F. Kennedy's motorcade in Dallas.

I rushed to the studio where a noontime local show was on the air and broke in to report that the president had been shot. As I rushed by, a sour old station technician actually said to me, "It's about time someone got the SOB." One of my colleagues pulled me away as I lunged toward the jerk.

I remember thinking in my twenty-three-year-old innocence, "This doesn't happen in America." It was just the beginning. At the end of that dark weekend, my life, Meredith's, and the world were forever changed.

The Omaha experience did come with a bonus for Meredith and me. Somehow one of the most prestigious stations in the country, WSB in Atlanta, heard about me and hired me in 1965 as the anchor of the 11:00 P.M. news.

CHAPTER 13

Atlanta and NBC

IN ATLANTA, I was quickly in the midst of America's Civil Rights Movement and came to know brave young activists my age, such as John Lewis and Julian Bond, who were a new generation of Black leaders.

I made a point of arriving early at Atlanta's historic Ebenezer Baptist Church when Dr. King was in town to preach. I'll always remember King's father, Daddy King, seated behind his son, whispering loud enough for even those of us in the white folks' second story to hear: "Keep it simple, son, keep it simple."

Mother and Dad visited us, their first trip to the Deep South, but they were distracted by unsettling family news. My brother Mike's Marine outfit had just been given orders to ship out to Vietnam. After a year, he would make it home safely and begin a rewarding career as a Bell Telephone technician.

Meanwhile I was quickly thrust into the Southern upheaval over civil rights, often filling in until NBC could get network reporters to the scene of the latest confrontation. It remains one of the important passages of my lucky life. NBC took notice and offered me a job in its Los Angeles bureau.

Meredith and I began an odyssey that took us from Atlanta to NBC in Los Angeles, then Washington, and finally New York.

In the tumultuous 1960s, America was deeply divided by the war in Vietnam, and California was an epicenter of protest. I was one of NBC's correspondents covering the upheaval, from Berkeley to the riotous 1968 Democratic National Convention in Chicago. The nights and streets were war zones with the young in long hair and using scabrous language, flinging fecal bombs, warring with Chicago cops swinging nightsticks and electronic prods across Lincoln Park, all on national television. Covering it, I kept thinking, "This is the undoing of America. How the hell will it end up?"

What I didn't fully appreciate at the time is that the attacks on America by the young, many with draft deferments that exempted them from military service in Vietnam, played right into the fury of working-class Americans watching on television the protestors with their college deferments.

When it was over, I flew to Yankton for a family visit before going on to California, and I immediately got into an ugly shouting match with my father. He, too, hated the war, but he hated even more the attacks on working-class cops, many of whom likely had sons fighting in Vietnam. My brother Mike was just back from a year of duty as a Marine in Vietnam, where he had largely noncombatant duty, thank God. Dad and I had our worst father-son confrontation ever, and only later did I appreciate his understandable anger about the deep divisions between the privileged young and the working class.

For the next five years I covered the political chaos in California, and then in Washington starting in 1973. Richard Nixon and his closest aides were caught in one of America's darkest political scandals: Watergate. Their criminal behavior involved trying to fix the 1972 presidential election. I covered Nixon's final year in office as he contrived foreign trips in his ever more desperate attempts to hold off impeachment. But it was too late. His self-inflicted wounds and outrageously illegal schemes were fatal.

Watergate ignited profound changes in American political culture, beginning with the historic journalism of Bob Woodward, Carl Bernstein, and their legendary boss, Ben Bradlee. At the time there were only three women in the White House press corps, none of them as the primary reporters for one of the three major networks. Now there are women of all backgrounds in those roles, filling on-air, cable, and syndicated network roles.

I've always thought Meredith and our friend the late Cokie Roberts were emblematic of the transition for modern women. When we first met in California, Meredith and Cokie were both full-time moms and full-time professionals. Cokie was a leading voice for women in journalism, while also becoming a primary voice on public radio.

As Meredith and I moved across the country, we became advocates for Red and Jean to move to California, where brothers Bill and Mike were settling. We offered financial help for them to buy a two-bedroom condominium in an established development not too far from where Meredith's parents were spending winters.

Mother made it clear that they were able to make it on their own. She found a young, very smart financial adviser and began to build what turned out to be a modest but comfortable nest egg.

As for Dad, it would mean retiring from his beloved full-time job as foreman in charge of developing the recreational areas around Gavins Point Dam. He agreed and went to the appropriate office to file for retirement, but it was closed. He made another appointment but didn't keep it. Instead, he called me in tears—the first time I heard him cry. "I'm just not ready," he explained. "I love my job. I'd miss seeing the sun catch the snow off the big blades on the plow when there's a storm. Work has been my whole life." I understood, having watched him all these years go happily off to daily jobs and spend weekends working on family chores in his basement workshop or helping others with some vexing car problem.

I suggested he spend all of his unused vacation

time on a trip to Southern California and try things out in a rented condominium. Brother Mike would be nearby with their shared interest in household projects and leisure-time shopping at Trader Joe's, a very imaginative food store, or in big box stores such as Costco. It worked. Mother and Dad found a two-bedroom condominium in an established development with access to a workshop.

Dad became a convert to the year-round sunshine and the snow-free recreational opportunities. Mother signed up for trips to the Los Angeles Philharmonic or plays at the Chandler Pavilion. She became an ardent fan of the California Angels baseball team and the Los Angeles Lakers of Kobe Bryant fame.

I took them to the NBC studios to meet my friend Redd Foxx, an African American comedian famous for his scatological sense of humor. When I introduced Red Brokaw to Redd Foxx, Foxx got wide-eyed and said "**Red** Brokaw! I'm Redd too. I'll bet we're related!" That's a story that made its way back to Bristol in a hurry.

Meredith's parents were in the same California neighborhood, and her father worked out a deal with Red. They'd trade Dr. Auld's workshop time for Red's gardening allotment.

In the evening Red would like to take a drink out on his patio and say, "If the boys in Bristol could see me now."

Then, as my NBC News contract was running out and I was fortuitously being recruited by ABC, CBS, and my friend Ted Turner at CNN, some astronomical salary speculation began to appear in the press. Red noticed and called. After needling me about not having on NBC a news item he had heard from Paul Harvey, the hugely popular longtime national radio broadcaster, he got into the salary issue.

"Is this true?" he asked.

"Dad, we've never talked money before. Why start now?"

"Well," he answered, "when you were growing up you always ran a little short at the end of the month. I need to know how much I have to put aside this time."

We both had a big laugh.

It was our last conversation.

CHAPTER 14

Saddle Up for
the Trip Ahead

A WEEK LATER, when I was attending a **Nightly News** planning session in Washington, Meredith called.

"Red had a heart attack at home and he's been rushed to the hospital."

"He's going to be okay, isn't he?" I asked.

It didn't look good.

Nooooo! He was sixty-nine and in the best years of his life. Now, suddenly, Red had met a challenge he couldn't overcome.

We all agreed that the funeral would be in Yankton and Dad would be buried in the cemetery next to Mother's parents, Grandpa Jim and Grandma Ethel, facing west toward the Missouri River.

The funeral filled the large Yankton Congregational Church with blue-collar craftsmen from Red's work crews, Main Street merchants, fellow members of the Elks lodge, physicians, his favorite Chevy dealer, Yankton pals of Bill and Mike, and my college friends. The North Dakota ranchers made the long drive down for the service but had to get right back for their evening and next-morning chores.

At the service my brother Bill summed up Red's life and his standing with those who came to honor him when he observed, "Dad was like a new fallen oak tree. A little rough on the outside but inside, smooth and sturdy."

The burial was on a blustery, cold winter day in Yankton's cemetery. It was so appropriate. The South Dakota winter; nearby, the grave of Mother's parents, who had given Jean permission to go on that first date with Red; the snowy prairie unfolding to the west; Dad's friends from the Elks lodge as a kind of honor guard.

Back at the church for the traditional post-burial luncheon, a college roommate entered wide-eyed and summoned me to his side. "You're not gonna believe this," he said, "I was listening to Paul Harvey on the way from the cemetery and his last item was about your father!"

Harvey had ended his broadcast by saying Red Brokaw was being buried today in Yankton, South Dakota, a Corps of Engineers foreman who worked on Gavins Point Dam.

He went on, "Next week Red Brokaw's son Tom will become the co-anchor of **NBC Nightly News**."

Later, I called Mr. Harvey to thank him and ask what prompted him to do the story.

He said, "It's a great American story. Your father,

a successful blue-collar Corps of Engineers foreman, has a son who is about to take one of the most important jobs in American journalism. Only in America!"

"Mr. Harvey," I said, "my dad was a huge fan of your broadcasts and was always reminding me of stories you did that we did not on **NBC Nightly News**. With your tribute, he had the last word."

At the end of the day of Dad's funeral, I took his car and began driving aimlessly west along the Missouri River. It was his kind of day—cold with deep snow. I came to a remote ranch where a cowboy was trying to corral a stubborn steer and head him through a gate. I stopped to watch as the steer evaded the cowboy time after time. Finally, the cowboy cornered the steer and drove him through the gate, looking at me and laughing, as if to say, "What the hell!"

I loved every aspect of that metaphorical moment.

As I drove away in his car, I wished Red had been with me—and then I realized he was. I could hear his laugh and see the shake of his head. We had shared this last day on the prairie together, just as the sun was setting and the cowboy was riding to the barn.

Sixty-nine years after his birth in his mother's wrought-iron bed at home, after his childhood of hard work and deprivation, after his unlikely courtship and marriage to Mother, his discovery of an inner genius for machinery—which led to a life of blue-collar financial security and social esteem—his American life had come to an end.

As his idol Paul Harvey would say, "And now you know the rest of the story."

Following Dad's death, Mother stayed the course in California.

It was not always easy. Brother Mike remembers Mother coming to his house the first Christmas after Dad was gone. She got out of her car with presents in hand and then realized something was missing. That redhead who had been part of her life since she was seventeen. Mike said she turned around, went back to the car, and sat there until he retrieved her.

Mother continued to visit us in New York, where she chatted with Walter Cronkite one night at the theater. My favorite exchange involved our friend Nora Ephron, the celebrated journalist, screenwriter, essayist, and everyone's smart-set hostess.

When I introduced Mother to Nora, Mother immediately said, "We've met before—at that Tommy Tune show on Broadway."

Nora said, "Uh, I didn't see the Tommy Tune show."

Mother immediately said, "Yes you did!"

Nora laughed and said, "Okay, I did," telling me later: "I didn't, but I so loved your mother's certainty I wasn't going to argue."

Nora would always ask how Mother was doing, and when she was in town, we'd make sure their paths would cross.

In California, Mother met a winning companion in her bridge group, and they became a couple. He had been an animator for Disney, and although he was different from Dad, they shared a creative gene and an obvious affection for Mother. Mother's life was the one she always deserved, and she approached it with Midwestern manners and sensibility.

A family friend published a popular Orange County magazine, and he arranged a lunch for Mom and the mothers of Steve Martin and Diane Keaton, all local residents. He knew Mom well and thought she would be the easiest guest. Wrong. Mother had watched me all those years and knew that the best insurance for a no-harm interview was to be an active subject.

The editor laughed when he told me that Steve Martin's and Diane Keaton's moms were no problem. He said, "Jean, your mom, wanted to go over quotes and conclusions."

As a schoolgirl, Mother had wanted to be a journalist. Instead, she became an active Democrat wherever we lived, volunteering to canvass neighborhoods for the party at election time and taking a larger role in the Senate campaign of South Dakota's last Democratic senator, Tom Daschle.

I have a vivid memory of my mother waking me up early the morning after the 1948 presidential election, when the Democratic incumbent Harry Truman was thought to have no chance against Thomas Dewey, a New York prosecutor.

Truman, the feisty Missouri man of the Midwest, went after Dewey in a no-holds-barred whistle-stop tour of heartland America, and won in a historic upset. Mother was overjoyed, saying, "We won, we won!" I have always counted that morning as the beginning of my lifelong journalistic passion for politics.

In California, I invited Mom to the dedication of the Richard Nixon Library, which I was covering years after Nixon had resigned in disgrace. I asked her if she wanted to meet the former president, for whom she'd never voted. She did, and they immediately fell into a lively conversation. Mother knew that the president's wife, Pat, had lived in South Dakota's Black Hills, where her father was a gold miner.

They also shared the Depression experience, the war years, and postwar years. I'd never seen Nixon so relaxed with a stranger. When we walked away, I teased her, saying I would tell all of her Democratic party friends about her Nixon encounter.

She laughed and said, "Well, I still wouldn't vote for him, but I enjoyed that."

Her California life was a long way from that one-room schoolhouse, failing farm, and the uncertain future she faced when she was coming of age.

But when asked if she ever felt bitter in those difficult days she said, "Of course not. We were all in it together. You got up and did the best you could and the next day and the next."

That was Mother's creed all the rest of her life. She

took advantage of new opportunities in California, but the fundamental values she developed in her formative years never left.

She was also up for new adventures. When she visited us in Montana, she wanted to go on a river trip, even though she couldn't swim. We bundled her into a pair of life jackets, and it all went well. At the end we took her to a legendary bar called Road Kill Cafe, positioned her on a barstool and watched as a local cowboy ordered a shot of whiskey and slid it down to her. Without hesitation, Mother picked it up and knocked it back.

As she was an Angels baseball fan, I took her to a game in Anaheim where she could watch from her wheelchair in an elevated section. I noticed she was looking around at the fans in the expensive seats, and when I asked if she was okay, she answered, "Yes, but how do all these people afford these tickets? My god, they're so expensive."

She was also a big Los Angeles Lakers fan. I asked Kobe Bryant if he'd mind sending her an autographed Lakers poster. She proudly displayed it in her bedroom until he was accused of sexual assault by a Colorado hotel employee who was showing him to his room. Mother took down the poster and slid it beneath her bed. Later, when Bryant apologized for his behavior, she put the poster back up.

She even went to a Lakers game at the Forum in Los Angeles. Lakers officials placed her with team wives, who were cordial but puzzled. Who was this grandmotherly white lady? When she explained, they welcomed her to their exclusive club and made sure she had all she needed.

Alas, that night she developed a serious hip affliction, and when she returned home her mobility was so greatly compromised that she was confined to bed most of the time. It was clear the end was drawing near.

Mike, his wife Beth, and Mari Tolsa, who took care of Mom, were at her bedside the night those of us in New York were being honored by the International Rescue Committee, a global human rights organization formed in the 1930s to assist Jews fleeing Europe. The IRC has long been a family favorite global aid program, so it was especially fitting that we were backstage when we heard Mom was fading fast.

Our daughter Sarah Brokaw spoke for the family on stage, expressing our gratitude for the honor, especially on a night when we were thinking of the matriarch, Grandma Jean, who inspired us all to be compassionate and grateful for the opportunity to help others. We rushed home just in time to hear from Mike in California.

Jean Conley Brokaw died just shy of her ninety-fourth birthday, after a life of hardship and compassion. She was loved by her family and a vast circle of friends from the prairie to the shores of California; she was a mother, grandmother, and citizen—endlessly curious, opinionated but never mean-spirited.

Later, as we gathered in our New York living room,

we wept and laughed, remembering her strength in managing three sons and a construction foreman husband, her prominent place in the lives of daughters-in-law and grandchildren, her humanity and compassion. And we all agreed her timing was perfect. She waited until she got a shout-out at the Waldorf ballroom before she left us.

At her burial in Yankton next to Red, we kept the ceremony simple, as she would have wanted it. Our middle granddaughter read from **Little House on the Prairie,** Laura Ingalls Wilder's classic novel based on her family's pioneering days eighty miles from where Grandma Jean had grown up.

We had the reception at a historic church founded by freed slaves who made their way north on the Mississippi and Missouri rivers to Yankton following the Civil War. That choice raised a few eyebrows, but in our family we knew that Mother would have approved.

EPILOGUE

Red and Jean and their American Dream is a tale that is not confined to these two children of the prairie during traumatic times. They were not alone in their struggles, nor were they alone in their determination to constantly confront challenges—in wartime and in peacetime—and to prevail.

Their generation was not perfect, but it took on the Great Depression and a world war, and it began to address the injustices of social and racial discrimination—a struggle that continues to this day.

Now that generation is gone, and America is faced with the consequences of Covid-19, an insidious global organic invasion, at a time when the instruments of common cause are greatly strained. We're a society with so much more money and so many more parts, interests, cultures, and international challenges. We're more divided ideologically than at any time since the Civil War. I say that not casually, but because as a journalist of some standing, I never expected to see a president so determined to launch a revolution against the results of an election that indisputably rejected him.

Jean and Red and their American Dream was a different time in America and the world. Yet they met the challenge without whining or whimpering. I never heard either of them complaining that life was not fair. Instead, they gave us, their successors, the will to go on. During these very troubled times, I think of them and their generation often, and I thank God for their enduring legacy of quiet courage and common persistence. From the prairie to the California coast, from hard times to war, from peace and prosperity to retirement and world travel, they stayed steady and true to the values of their families and the promise that better days would be their reward.

In a new century, the world faces threats not just from a new war or famine but from an invisible, deadly, and cunning virus that continues to reignite as a terrifying threat.

The American Dream remains an uneven light in these days of sharp differences. We wonder: Is that goal of a "more perfect Union" achievable? Yet the American ideal remains a goal, a work in progress not yet fully realized, mankind challenged anew by an unprecedented global virus epidemic and a greatly fractured American political structure.

We are a country more divided than unified. The tools of mass communication are in many hands

Gavins Point Dam

and too often with conflicting aims. We'll never be a perfectly united country. In the past, through wars and social and economic upheaval, this historic and unique collection of goals and interests has found imperfect but enduring common cause. From 1776 to the twenty-first century, we have struggled, made mistakes, prevailed, taken in new Americans, and we remain in search of that more perfect union against ever greater odds.

What has not faltered is the American Dream of Red, Jean, and all the people who were born here, moved here, fought for their place as citizens. These Americans represent an ever-wider range of backgrounds, beliefs, and hopes. They cling to their passions and certainties, too many with a blindness that threatens us all.

In a new century we are indebted to those who went before, and we hope we can measure up to their legacy. The American system of laws and traditions is a unique and vibrant form of governance, constantly challenged and renewed.

May it always endure.

ACKNOWLEDGMENTS

What I quickly learned when I first started writing books is that no man is an island, and that essential truth remains comforting.

This book depends heavily on memories left behind by my parents and their friends, as well as the documentation of formal history accounts of their time.

It also depends on the sharp eyes of Kate Medina, the legendary Random House editor who first encouraged me to write and has been at my side for nine books. My gratitude knows no bounds.

The same is true for the peerless Random House team. I am especially grateful to Gina Centrello for her friendship and her extraordinary leadership. I am grateful for the careful work of Andy Ward, Rachel Rokicki, Benjamin Dreyer, Carole Lowenstein, Dennis Ambrose, Steve Messina, Rebecca Berlant, Leah Sims, Evan Camfield. Also for the expertise of Lucas Heinrich, Robbin Schiff, Louisa McCullough, Monica Rae Brown.

The personal captain of Team Brokaw is Geri Jansen, who first came to work for me fresh out of college. We've been side-by-side on nine books, through her marriage to Mike and the growth of their family of son Tommy and daughter Kelsey. On both sides, we see this as an extended family.

Finally, to Mother and Dad, undying gratitude for lives well lived, from the hardships of the Great Depression to the security of middle-class prosperity. The three Brokaw boys weren't models of pristine behavior, but Mother and Dad knew where to draw lines.

Finally, a shout-out to America's unending pursuit of better lives for all.

PHOTO CREDITS

57   Courtesy of the Brokaw family
62   Jim Lo Scalzo / EPA-EFE / Shutterstock
65   Adobe Stock Images / Patrick Ziegler
69   U.S. Army Corps of Engineers photo
      furnished courtesy of Pickstown and Fort
      Randall Museum
72   Courtesy of the Brokaw family
74   U.S. Army Corps of Engineers photo
      furnished courtesy of Pickstown and Fort
      Randall Museum
75   U.S. Army Corps of Engineers photo
      furnished courtesy of Pickstown and Fort
      Randall Museum
77   U.S. Army Corps of Engineers
79   U.S. Army Corps of Engineers photos
      furnished courtesy of Pickstown and Fort
      Randall Museum (all)
97   Harry Weddington, U.S. Army Corps
      of Engineers
99   Jim Wark
101   Adobe Stock Images / Patrick Ziegler
102   © Jerry L Mennenga, www.lostinsiouxland.com
      (top); Pat Hansen, www.PatHansenPhotos.com
      (bottom)
104   Courtesy of the Yankton County Historical
      Society Photo Collection, Yankton, SD (top);
      U.S. Army Corps of Engineers photo
      furnished courtesy of Pickstown and Fort
      Randall Museum (bottom)
133   U.S. Army Corps of Engineers

ABOUT THE AUTHOR

TOM BROKAW is the author of seven bestsellers. He joined NBC News in 1966. From 1976 to 1981 he anchored **Today** on NBC. From 1983 to 2008 he was the anchor of **NBC Nightly News with Tom Brokaw**. He has won every major broadcast journalism award. In 2014 Brokaw was awarded the Presidential Medal of Freedom.

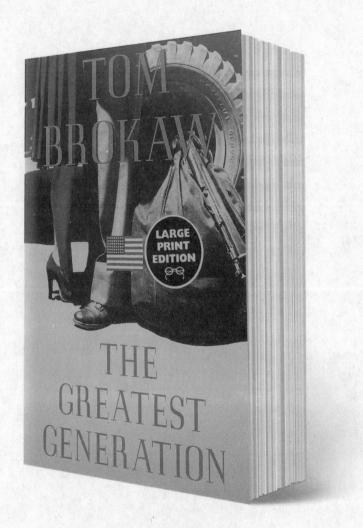